A BOOK OF
MIRACLES

A BOOK OF MIRACLES

Contributed by the students
of the Very Right Reverend
Dr. Lewis S. Bostwick

*Edited By Susan Hull Bostwick and the
Book of Miracles Committee*

DEJA VU BOOK COMPANY
SAN RAFAEL, CA 94901
1987

A Deja Vu Book.

Published by Deja Vu Book Company.
A Division of Deja Vu Publishing Company.
1314 Lincoln Ave., San Rafael, CA 94901

This collection of miracle stories is the product of a year's work by the Book of Miracles Committee of the Church of Divine Man: Rt. Rev. Susan Hull Bostwick, Rev. Paula Camacho, Rev. Margaret Davis, Rev. Charlene Hubbard, Rev. John Huddleston, Rev. Jennifer Kimberley, Rev. Dona Wessells.

Design and art direction by Rev. Dona Wessells.
Illustration and calligraphy by Rev. Margaret Davis.

Published in hard and soft cover.

Published in the United States of America.

Library of Congress Catalog Card Number: 87-71086.

ISBN: 0-943341-00-0 24.95 (cloth)
ISBN: 0-943341-01-9 9.95 (paper)

This book is a collection of miracles as expressed by the individual authors and is in no way diagnosing or prescribing medicine or a substitute for sound medical advice.

ACKNOWLEDGEMENTS

The creation of this collection of miracles—the computer type-setting, art, editing—has been a labor of love and dedication. It was inspired by the Very Right Rev. Lewis S. Bostwick himself. During the past 13 years at the Berkeley Psychic Institute, Lewis has put out the word: "You don't even recognize your miracles; when are you going to put all these miracles into a book? We create so many miracles that we become complacent about them and no one knows what a great thing has been done."

It was done largely through the cooperation and determination of volunteers giving hundreds of hours: Rt. Rev. Susan Hull Bostwick, Rev. Paula Camacho, Rev. Margaret Davis, Rev. Charlene Hubbard, Rev. John Huddleston, Rev. Jennifer Kimberley, Rev. Dona Wessells have been the mainstays of making this book happen. And of course, it could not have been the dream that Lewis asked for without the contributors whose names appear on the stories. Much appreciation also goes to the many "service tithers" who input copy, to the staff of Deja Vu Publishing Company and to the staff of the Berkeley Psychic Institute and the Church of Divine Man, who healed the invalidation that said it couldn't be done. This accomplishment is a miracle unto itself.

DEDICATION

The collection here is meant as a gift, a token of appreciation to the one person who created the psychic kindergarten named the Berkeley Psychic Institute and the Church of Divine Man, Lewis S. Bostwick. He is the archbishop of the church, and the teacher and healer who set the energy level of an expectation of miracles. He has taught us amusement and neutrality and cajoled and chided us into liking ourselves. He has taught us how to find that special place of communication with the cosmic and the human soul. We have been taught the value of the validation of spirit to spirit hellos and that nothing in this world is worth exchanging for that attainment. Words of thanks cannot express the gratitude that is felt here for the work that he has done. Let it suffice that this book, which includes the stories of the healers who helped create the miracles and who are Lewis Bostwick's staff and students, will be that message.

CONTENTS

TALKING TO SPIRIT

REBIRTH

INTRODUCTION

Man has been looking for answers to the universe and his relationship to the cosmos since his beginning. To a psychic, or someone aware of himself as spirit, the answer may lie in the ability to heal or the certainty to follow his intuition. The search for truth is not merely a mystical exercise practiced by the religious: journalists look for it in man's deeds and words and scientists look for it in test tubes. The seeker looks within.

Learning to listen to the "inner voice" can be an adventurous task—leading to the discovery of the unknown and even the god of one's own heart. The writers here are expressing their own individual inner search. They all have had a mystical, life-changing experience, something that happened during their private search for truth that cannot be easily analyzed by science. The experience in some instances was magical; in others astounding; in all unexplainable in everyday language. We label these occurrences miracles for want of any better words. But amazing, spectacular, wondrous and wonderful all fit nicely.

The people whose stories appear in this book studied at the Berkeley Psychic Institute, a kindergarten sanctuary where sensitive people can learn simple psychic tools to help them in their search. They use a lexicon that has not been put in any dictionary yet: I am in a "growth period"; I can have my "own space" and I sense the angry "energy"; my "havingness" was "invalidated" and I needed some "grounding"; I was "amused" at all the "competition pictures." These words are part of a psychic lingo that has developed. You will read about the psychic tools of "protection roses," "center of head," "running energy." No one has standardized how one should talk about psychic phenomenon when it is being acted out through a human being.

To someone listening to a budding clairvoyant at the Berkeley Psychic Institute the conversation could appear foreign and non-sensical: "I was blowing up roses when I lost my grounding, got stuck on an invalidation picture and trashed myself for not pulling my girlfriend's cords out of my second chakra." However, the reader should not be dismayed: we have put together a small glossary in the back of the book.

The writers present these stories as their personal vignettes, slices of their lives that for some have gone unmentioned until now; for others the miracle was broadcast to friends far and wide. All came into the Berkeley Psychic Institute for a healing or an aura reading, or a stop along the road to finding the meaning of life. These stories refer to the experiences they had during this stop.

The miracle may have occurred at a Healing Clinic, Beginning Meditation Class, Beginning Healing Class, a weekly Psychic Demonstration, in the Clairvoyant Program or while one was courageously practicing the psychic skills being taught. Thus the book is divided into chapters to define the kinds of psychic experiences one may have through the Berkeley Psychic Institute: My First Hello; Talking to Spirit; Healing; Rebirth; Creating Your Own Reality; On the Astral; Using the Tools.

My First Hello—"You are not just your body; you are spirit," the reader said. This communication has the ability to create a multitude of miracles, a spiritual breakthrough and one very big growth period. The first aura reading can be a dramatic experience in being validated as a capable being.

Talking to Spirit—What happens when you answer the ringing in the ears with a "Hello, who are you and what do you want?" Talking to spirit can be a healing for both ends of the line. Spirit likes communication. When you have a conversation with spirit, somebody gets a healing.

Healing—Medical invalidation (you are not in charge of your body, the doctor is) has caused many people to find the doorstep of the Berkeley Psychic Institute. What has attracted people to psychic healing is its simplicity and that it works. You are the creator of your own healing miracle.

Rebirth—Having a breakthrough spiritual experience, something that turns your life around 180 or 360 degrees, can cause you to come into your body in a completely new way, seeing the world with a clearer, wider window.

Creating Your Own Reality—When you are the master of your

own universe, you create and destroy what you want: more havingness for money, spiritual growth, happiness, communication and even miracles.

On the Astral—What happens when you leave the body? Out of body experiences can be tremendous healing adventures.

Using the Tools—Honing and owning psychic tools such as grounding, running life force energy, finding the center of your head, creating and destroying mental image pictures can lead to a miracle—either for yourself or another—at work or at home. Once you own them, honing them is the key.

Two of the keys to these miracles manifesting are amusement and non-resistance: the body and spirit were ready for change. Some level of enthusiasm had been reached when the change occurred with apathy, boredom and anger being left behind. Why did these miracles occur at the Berkeley Psychic Institute and not some other place? Here, miracles are an unspoken expectation: they are a daily occurrence, in a world where one hopes and prays for one miracle a lifetime. The Institute attracts special people, sensitives who have spent most of their lives unconsciously healing those around them. When taught to direct and control that tremendous power, miracles occur as evidenced herein.

Susan Hull Bostwick

FIRST HELLOS

"You are not just your body; you are spirit," the reader said. This communication has the ability to create a multitude of miracles, a spiritual breakthrough and one very big growth period. The first aura reading can be a dramatic experience in being validated as a capable being.

1   *A FAIR BEGINNING*

t was a Sunday morning in October, 1984, and I was, as usual, reading my horoscope in the paper. That day my horoscope said something about using my psychic abilities. Didn't know I had any! As I flipped through the paper I saw a notice about a Psychic Fair being held that day in Fairfax. Well, that was too much of a coincidence—I had to go check this out.

At first I just walked around looking. Hundreds of people were sitting in pairs. The ones with their eyes closed were talking, and the ones with their eyes open were listening. Quite the opposite of most conversations I'd witnessed. Something was happening here!

I decided it was safe to get a palm reading. I sat down opposite a lady about my age who yawned and said she needed a minute to find her space. "Right!" I thought, as I watched her yawn some more and wave her hands through the air as though swatting flies. After a few minutes she began to "look" at my hand with her eyes closed, and she began to talk about colors she saw. I thought palm reading had to do with lines. She talked about how guilty I felt. "The funny thing," she said, "is that it's not your fault." And I began to cry. I felt silly crying—I didn't realize I was doing a good job of releasing energy.

After the reading I asked her a thousand questions. "How did you start this? How long have you been doing this? What do the colors look like to you? Were you different before you became psychic?" She answered my questions patiently and in amusement, then directed me to the healing booth. After my healing I got a Female Reading, and cried during that reading too. My reader talked about things I couldn't believe anyone could know.

Then I remember Lewis came up to me and said hello, and set up a full two hour aura reading.

Something WAS happening here. Something was different— and I was different. I had been said hello to for the first time in my life.

Rev. Cindy Dunn

HELLO, GOD, ARE YOU THERE?

There was a time when I was not a happy person. According to societal standards, I should have been—I had a career as a pediatric nurse practitioner, a husband, a house in Marin County, two cars in the garage and one a BMW. I had a beautiful infant son. And we had a 40' sailboat. We sailed, skied, took vacations in Mexico. I was supposed to have it all— but something was missing. I felt I was just going through the motions of living.

One day, I was picking up a friend's child at her daycare center. Jeanette, who ran the center, was very calm and certain. The children were all so happy and content at this center—much different from what I had seen at other daycares. I found myself sticking around to chat with her. I wanted to know how she was doing it . . . six children in one room and all happy and content. This woman had something to teach me.

We began to talk and I asked her how she got into running a daycare center. She told me her story of creating the center to meet two of her own needs—first, a job for herself, as she had never worked and was recently divorced; and second, a babysitting situation for her daughter, two-year-old Jenny.

I complimented her on how calm her center was, even with six kids running around. She looked at me and said, "You know, you've been making a lot of changes lately and I think you might enjoy a psychic reading."

"Enjoy"—the word stuck in my ears and echoed through my head. What was happening here? This was very odd—how did she know that I was making changes? I was a stranger to her. And even odder—how did she know that I was looking for something to enjoy?

Just the night before, with my son asleep and my husband still at work, I had sat down and begun to talk to myself. I had already tried to talk to my friends about being "disillusioned with it all" and they hadn't heard or understood. They had simply said, "You have everything. What could be missing? Don't be stupid!"

So I was sitting there, talking to myself, looking out the window as the light grew dimmer and the stars appeared. I sat there with my glass of wine—very good wine—talking to it as if it could hear me. "Is this all there is?" I said. "Houses, cars, dinner parties . . . I want something more—but what? And who can tell me?" I laughed—my friends didn't have any answers, so who did? I decided to talk to God—if there was one, and I wasn't sure about that. "God, is this all there is? Is this some cosmic joke of yours?" I laughed even more; the idea of talking to a wine glass and to God! I must be crazy! Then I said, "Well, God, if this is all there is, I'm going to the bridge and I'm going to jump off, unless you show me right away that there's something more to living . . ." And I laughed and laughed.

• • • • •

Well, I knew that Jeanette's communication to me was on a new level that I had never received before. She told me about the Berkeley Psychic Institute and the following week, I went in and had my first psychic reading. I was astounded. Those five people who didn't know me from Adam, told me all about myself, my "disillusionment," about my talking to God and asking for this kind of spiritual communication. Through the whole reading, I held my breath. They even had to remind me to breathe. Someone was finally seeing who I really was and what I wanted. It was a very big HELLO to me the spirit.

I left that reading in total joy. I skipped down the street, knowing that I had received something really tremendous. I didn't know what those psychic readers had, but whatever it was, I wanted it.

I now understand what is meant by "What if a man gain the whole world and lose his own soul . . ." I had gained the world and nearly lost my soul in the process. Today, I have my own enthusiasm and an awareness of who I am as a spirit free and eternal, creating through my physical body. That first hello was an incredible miracle—it changed my whole life.

Rev. Shane Smith

A WEEKEND OF HELLOS

he first time I arrived at the Berkeley Psychic Institute was on a sunny Saturday afternoon in the spring of 1981. Little did I know how dramatically each of the next three days would change my life.

For years I had been searching for answers on how to develop my psychic abilities and had read most of the books available on the subject: Seth, Jess Stearn, est, L. Ron Hubbard, Ledbetter, etc. I had also taken Tarot workshops, hypnosis classes, past life regression seminars, intuition workshops, Gestalt therapy, and I was doing automatic writing.

An eight-year relationship had just ended and I was still recovering. My ears rang constantly and the doctors simply commented on what beautiful eardrums I had, which, needless to say, didn't do much to stop the ringing. I was depressed and in survival. Doing affirmations was helping a little bit, but I knew there was a lot more that I could do for myself, if I just knew what it was!

Then a friend called to tell me about the Berkeley Psychic Institute in Sacramento, and that they had free healing clinics on Saturday afternoons. I grabbed my two roommates and headed over there.

When I walked through the door of that beautiful old house, Rev. Michael Kolak, the healing teacher, came up and said hello. This was not just another hello directed to my body; he said hello to me, the spirit in the body; (or in my case, actually, to me, the spirit who was trying to get into my body!) He sat me down and proceeded to wave his hands around me, telling me how he had healing guides who plugged into his hands and worked through him to take foreign energy out of my body and aura. He also described to me what he saw them working on, and he mentioned all the spirits without bodies that were living in my aura and using my body. He commented that if my ears were ringing, it was the beings trying to communicate to me. I had not told him my ears always rang! I also remember him saying that most of my energy at that time was covered over with black uck that wasn't allowing me the freedom to create for myself or have any fun.

That healing felt very good, and everything he said made total sense to me: it all fit. It gave me a lot of answers and a feeling that here I could find my niche. I signed up for an aura reading the following Monday; but I couldn't wait, so I went down to a psychic fair at the BPI of Berkeley on Sunday. There I had four readings: Spirit Guide, Female, Aura, and Money. More hellos, more validation for my abilities as spirit in a body. And I wanted still more! After my two-hour aura reading on the Monday, I signed up for my first class.

Now, almost six years later, I enjoy teaching students how to read auras and say hello to all those people out there who are also spirits in bodies. It is fun to watch others as I give them a spiritual hello.

Rev. Aurelia Scherf

GOODBYE GURU

or ten years I was with a guru. For ten years, I also suffered from headaches, dizziness and nausea. I went to many doctors for this but they could find no explanation for it and summed it up as "stress."

Eventually I found myself at the Berkeley Psychic Institute and one evening, Lewis gathered all the Clairvoyant students together after class and gave me a healing.

"Do you know what your problem is?" he asked.

"No," I said, my attention fixed on his quizzical smile.

"You're an out-of-control trance medium!" he said, "Like most of these people here."

There were about twenty students sitting around, all with their eyes closed and yawning, and at this, they all laughed.

I was none the wiser and my head hurt, so I didn't laugh. But I felt safe.

"Have you been studying with a spiritual teacher, a guru?" Lewis asked me kindly.

"Yes."

"He has a big, fat cord right into your crown chakra. Would you like me to remove it for you?"

"Yes, please." Lewis made some movements around my head with his hands. Suddenly I felt a great rush of energy through my whole body and for a minute I thought I was going to pass out, it was so strong.

"Can you feel that energy coming back to you?" Lewis asked. "That guru was taking your energy." He continued working with his hands. "You've been around those street drugs, haven't you?" he said. "I'm going to repair some of the parts of your brain where those drugs have destroyed connections." As he worked, I felt the inside of my head expand and clear out. A wonderful, happy feeling came over me.

"That's your own energy!" said Lewis. I glanced cautiously around the room and saw that some of the students had opened their eyes and were looking at me with interest.

"She looks a bit different, doesn't she," chuckled Lewis. More students opened their eyes and I felt that they were actually seeing me, not just looking at my body.

"She's in her body now," said Lewis.

I began to cry. For the first time in my twenty-eight years, someone was saying hello to me.

From that night on, I've had no more of the pain, dizziness or nausea.

Rev. Donna Greer

1   THE DRAGON AND THE BRIGHT LIGHT

was standing on the porch of a small Victorian with light blue trim, on a neat, quiet Berkeley street. Next to me, my sister, Eileen, stood looking inquiringly at me. "Think we should knock again?" she asked. It was a sunny August afternoon and the birds were singing in the warm air. Before I had arrived, I had imagined a huge building bustling with scientific energy. I looked in confusion at this sunny little house. The Berkeley Psychic Institute? Maybe we had the wrong address.

Suddenly the door swung open and my fist knocking on the door was headed straight for an old woman's face. "What do you want?" she said loudly and shrilly, looking suspiciously at my fist as it lowered itself uncertainly.

"Is this the Berkeley Psychic Institute?" I asked, my hope fading.

"Why do you want to know?" she demanded.

By now, I knew we had the wrong place. "Well, I'm visiting from Los Angeles and wanted to stop by."

"Well, it is the Berkeley Psychic Institute, and no one is here yet. Come back later." She shut the door.

I shrugged my shoulders and we retreated down the steps.

I did not know at the time that that woman was the Very Rt. Rev. Dr. Lewis Bostwick's mother. I had met the proverbial dragon at the door, the one that guards the secrets of wisdom. Actually, she lived on the first floor and the BPI occupied the second floor. My sister and I had just interrupted her favorite soap opera.

When we returned later that evening, the house was ablaze with lights. People were sitting on the front steps talking and joking. They all looked perfectly normal, although very self-possessed. They were laughing and relaxed. I liked watching them have such a good time.

As I was led upstairs to the second floor, I was introduced to a balding, heavy-set man who had honest, piercing blue eyes. When he said hello to me, I felt that everything was going to be all right. I felt as if I was stepping up to a whole new level. He laughed at my expression and said, "Let me show you around."

In one room was a trance medium, who made me think of Jane Roberts with Seth, and he explained how this worked. We visited other rooms and watched people getting psychic readings. The information that spilled casually out of him made my head spin. Even more incredible was the everyday way that people were listening to him, making adjustments at his suggestion, and saying, "Oh, yes, that's much better. Now I can see the past-life picture in his fifth layer. . . ." I felt as if I had walked into the future or been transported onto the Starship Enterprise for the first time.

And yet everyone was so relaxed and happy. Even the few people who were having a hard time seemed to be relishing it. Later, as I spoke to Lewis, he said "Let me show you something." He had me sit in a chair and he stood behind me and began to press on my forehead in several different places. He said, "There have been so many people in your awareness, it's time to clear the counter top off so that you can start to communicate with yourself."

As he started to work on me on an energy level, a bright light started to appear in the center of my head. It was soft, bright, golden, and very comforting. "This is a miracle," I thought. "Like the birth of a planet." I sat silently with my eyes closed, watching the light shine in my head. I was enjoying this special moment. I heard Lewis say, "Do you see that bright light?" "Yes, I do," I said. How did he know? But there wasn't any time to wonder, as he was speaking again and I didn't want to miss anything. "That bright light is you. Say hello to that light," he said. I did and it answered back, "Hello!" Total happiness washed over me!

"Say, 'I love you,' " Lewis said.

"I love you," I said, a little self-consciously, to the bright light.

"I love you too," said the bright light, and I knew I had found my beginning.

Rt. Rev. Karen Tamura

"L" TELEPATHIC COMMUNICATION

ida I have to talk to you!" It was my living companion of eight years, calling me on the telephone after a year of separation. We met for dinner in a tiny cafe in Hayward, California. Over ribs and beer, Bill related his experience of having an aura reading at the Berkeley Psychic Institute.

"They told me there is a very psychic woman whose energy surrounds me and whose psychic abilities I have invalidated for years! The readers described you!"

Me psychic? I was thrilled! I had experienced telepathic communications and had had insights in the past, but rarely admitted it. Now, this man, an atheist scientist to whom I had looked for love and acceptance for most of my adult life, was passing on the most significant recognition of my existence (and without believing or understanding it himself.)

I called the Berkeley Psychic Institute the next morning and was invited to a free demonstration that afternoon. I did not mention Bill. Two psychic students sat in line before me and described the energy of an atheist man in my body, blocking my own use of my spiritual abilities. They described Bill! Then they removed his energy from my abdomen, spine and chest. Immediately I felt an intense warmth flowing upward from the base of my spine to my chest. One of the readers said, "Oh, are you aware that your kundalini just turned on?"

Was I ever! But wasn't it supposed to take lifetimes of meditation to turn on your kundalini? Here were all the promises of spirituality I had read of in the Tibetan masters—occurring to me within a two-hour time span in 1980 in Berkeley. I knew I wanted to gain control of my spiritual abilities for myself; and ever since then, I have been a student and teacher of psychic reading and healing.

Rev. Lida Eichenberger

NO, I DON'T LIKE UNICORNS!

"When I came in for an aura reading, I was afraid because this place, the Berkeley Psychic Institute, was a church. I had moved to California to go to school at U.C. Berkeley from a small, conservative town in Texas. I had always heard about psychics and was interested in going to see one, but I also had heard about weird churches and gurus who took your money and sent you to South America to commit suicide by drinking fruit punch! But my friend had survived a reading and told me it was very accurate. So I nervously agreed to try it.

The readers took me to a room and sat in line to read my aura. I was so skeptical that I didn't admit anything when they asked me questions. I just kept quiet. When they finished the first half and I went downstairs for the break, there was a short, oriental man talking to a black lady. I sat down and the man asked to look at the drawing of my aura. I said, "Sure," and gave it to him. After a minute, he gave it back to me and asked,

"Do you like unicorns?"
I said "No."
He said "Do you like to write?"
I said "Yes."

He said, "Do you like to write about unicorns?"

"No," I said.

Do you have unicorns in your room?"

"NO!" This guy is really off, I thought.

"Oh," he said, and walked out of the room.

Then he turned around and came back in and said "Because all I see when I look at you is a picture of a unicorn and you writing." He made a writing motion in the air. I shrugged.

Then suddenly I remembered that I had bought a diary with a unicorn on the cover. I didn't even like unicorns, but it had been the cheapest one on sale. "Oh, yeah!" I yelled. "There's a diary sitting next to my bed with a unicorn on it and I write in it every day!" He started laughing. Then I started laughing. I was amazed. This guy must really be psychic, I thought.

Then he said, "Who did you know who owned a ranch? You have horses in your aura." I admitted that I used to take care of some horses in Texas.

"You know," he said, "The reason your shoulders are slouched is because your grandmother told you to stand up straight all the time."

I said "Yeah, she did! I hated when she said that!"

"Yes, that's why you slouch your shoulders." He stood looking at me for a moment, then said "This month you will have three boyfriends. They are standing over your shoulder." I turned around to look, but I couldn't see anything. I laughed and stared back at him in awe.

"You can learn to do this, too," he said. "Just take a meditation class and find out. You can be more capable than I am."

Me? Be psychic? I laughed all the way upstairs for the rest of my reading. At the end, I signed up for Beginning Meditation Class. That man was Rt. Rev. Michael J Tamura.

Rev. Vessa Rhinehart

CUTTING THE
APRON STRINGS

eight years ago, when I first came to this country from France, I suffered from abdominal cramps and diarrhea. I had these symptoms daily for several months, and was in a great deal of pain and discomfort. My first reaction was to go to a doctor and find out what was wrong with my body. Well, after many tests and different opinions, I got the same answer from everybody: "Yes, you have a problem but we can find nothing that is creating it. So here is a prescription and we will see if this medication works." Well, I was not amused, and I also was not about to take any drugs without knowing why I was taking them.

I had heard through a friend about the Berkeley Psychic Institute and decided to go and have a psychic reading. This was a first for me and I was a little nervous about it. From all I had heard about psychics and fortune tellers, I was very skeptical as to their credibility. It was my last resort.

When I went to the BPI of Berkeley, four students were assigned to read me. Three were sitting in a straight line in front of me and the fourth was standing behind them. They were yawning and laughing and I was frozen on my chair. To my surprise, I found out a lot about many things: about what I was doing as a spirit in a body, why I had decided to visit this country, why I had left France and my family and friends. And above all, about why I was sick.

The readers described how my mother, who was worried about my traveling alone in this wild and crazy country, had put some of her protection energy in my space. Not wanting me to get hurt, she had covered my body with a white energy which kept other energies from getting in my body, but also kept my energy from flowing properly, and this was the cause of the problem.

I asked them to help me take my mother's energy out of my space and send it back to her. Right away, I felt a difference. Although I felt more vulnerable, there was a sense of great relief. For the next few hours, I felt a little disoriented, but the next day, I knew I was healed. The cramps were gone and I no longer had to run to the ladies' room every hour.

The readers had created a miracle, and being ready to be free of my mother's protection, I had allowed that miracle to happen. It *was a simple but powerful experience. I then understood that I too was psychic and could create miracles.*

Rev. Carmen Figueras

GETTING MY BACKBONE BACK

1 n 1977 I had my own cottage in Sydney, Australia, and my two small boys lived there with me. I published a book, danced in a professional folk-dance troupe and was a member of a women's collective which ran a refuge for battered women.

My ex-husband had taken himself off to Mexico in search of his roots. I had many friends and acquaintances—but was I happy? No way! I felt lost and confused and my back and neck hurt so much that I would black out if I had to stand still for more than a minute or so.

I instinctively knew doctors and chiropractors wouldn't provide any answers; and I found out that encounter groups and the women's movement couldn't either, nor could falling in love! What to do? I smoked weed and lay on the beautiful Sydney beaches, savoring (from six feet above my body) the crashing waves and hot sun.

I knew I needed meditation. The conviction grew in me that I would find it in Berkeley. So when my ex-husband turned up one day (still trailing no roots that I could see), I sent my seven-year-old over with him to Berkeley, sold my house, and with my four-year-old, took a plane over here myself.

We arrived on a Tuesday. That day, I said to my ex-husband, "It's your turn," and I kissed my boys goodbye for a year.

On Wednesday I wandered around, easing into my new condition of no home, job, friends or commitments. I was in pain and confusion, but so what? I had money and a purpose! I loafed into the occult bookstore on Telegraph Ave. There was a great variety of attractive books, but I picked up only one: "The Psychic Healing Book" by Amy Wallace. I opened it vaguely and out jumped "Berkeley Psychic Institute"! I closed it and asked the sales clerk if he knew where the Berkeley Psychic Institute was. "Oh, yeah," he said in boredom, and scribbled me a little map.

Five minutes later, when I walked in the door, I nearly turned and ran out again, so serene and poised was the woman who welcomed me. Exuding comfort, she smiled and invited me to look around. Her name was Mary and she was a graduate, she said. I saw (what I now know to have been) her glowing aura. She looked beautiful and I knew she had information that I wanted.

"I want to take a class," I blurted. Her eyes smiled at me with a secret amusement behind the courtesy. "Classes will be starting again in three weeks," she said. "Would you like an aura reading in the meantime?"

Three weeks! How could I last so long?

"Yes, please," I whispered.

On Friday, in my aura reading, when five people spent two and a half hours chuckling at me and congratulating me for "enjoying not enjoying it," I knew I had found the right place.

Over the subsequent months, I began learning to ground and run my energy. This started clearing the blocks from the energy channels along my spine. My adult height standing straight had been 5'7." In that first year, I grew to 5'9" and the back and neck pain disappeared.

My confusion changed to excitement: way in the most secret and certain part of me, I saw that I already knew the things they were teaching me! I saw what my problem was: I had been too nice! I had tried to believe my relatives and teachers so they wouldn't feel bad. I had lent them my space to strut around in. At every turn their faces frowned and scowled: "No, Jennifer! Be more ladylike! Don't laugh, this is serious! Wipe that smile off your face, young lady! Look at me when I'm speaking to you . . ."

Well, I'll look at you leaving, oh great relatives and teachers! Hello and goodbye. It's time to get off my back. This is my space and you've been trespassing! Trespassers will be exploded in a rose!

Rev. Jennifer Kimberley

1 WRONG NIGHT, RIGHT PLACE

heard about the Berkeley Psychic Institute of Santa Rosa from a co-worker who claimed to be a witch. Nevertheless, I decided to go to the Healing Clinic she mentioned. The day arrived, and the Healing Clinic was supposed to be at 7:00 p.m. My girlfriend, Anne, and I walked to the place, which was just a few blocks away, and knocked on the door.

A woman answered. "Can I help you?" she said.

"Yes, we understand that you have a free Healing Clinic tonight and we'd like to try one."

"Oh, well, the Healing Clinic was last night," said the woman. "We aren't doing healings tonight."

"Hello," piped a voice from behind the woman. "What can we do for you?" I explained to this round oriental man that we had come on the wrong night for a Healing Clinic and we would come back on the proper evening. But he beckoned us in, and asked the woman to give Anne a healing. "Come this way," he said to me.

I followed him into another room, where he sat me down and then sent for some students to come in and watch. He sat down across from me and started to tell me about all the yellow stuff that was around me (pot energy) and about my father. I was astounded at what he knew about me, when I had never seen him before. It was quite some time later when I noticed that the room was nearly full of people, most of them with their eyes closed and hands raised towards me. I felt that I had been sitting there talking and listening for hours. "Well and done," said the oriental man, who I later found out was Rt. Rev. Michael Tamura. "Hello!" It was as if a whole universe had opened before me. I knew that this was something very special and I felt so different; light and full of energy and very open and clean.

As I was led out of the room, I saw Anne reading a magazine and looking quite angry. "Where have you been for the last forty minutes?" she demanded.

I looked at her in wonder that so much time had passed. "I was getting a healing," I said. I realized that I had heard a hello from these psychics that she had not; I knew I would be back. . . .

Rev. Paul Siebert

FIRST AND A SECOND HELLO

a first hello that I enjoy remembering happened last year. One Friday night in August, having worked another action-packed week in the Church Office, I decided to walk up the road to the Berkeley Psychic Institute of Marin—the Seminary where I had received my Clairvoyant Training—to do an aura reading. I was excited about this reading—I felt it was going to be a very enjoyable and special one.

When I arrived at the Institute, the first person I saw was Patti, the sister of one of my friends. Patti was very pregnant and very tired of waiting. She was putting on a brave face but she looked rather worn down. So I started to laugh and joke with her about still waiting—she was approximately three weeks overdue—and I knew that I was going to be asked to read her that night.

We all sat down to run our energy. "Sue, I think I'd like you to read Patti," said Melissa, who was setting up the readings. "You can go upstairs in the front room."

As I looked at Patti clairvoyantly, all I could see were her family and friends, crowding her space with their wishes, hopes, concerns and expectations for the birth. Her parents, who live out of state, wanted her to be with them; her husband who had just been re-stationed many miles away in the Army, wanted her to be with him; and her two sisters wanted her to give birth here in the Bay Area with them. I talked to Patti about all these people and how their energy was adversely affecting her ability to give birth.

As I talked, I started to do a little healing work, helping her to move some of their energy outside of her space. Immediately she took a deep breath and settled more comfortably in her chair, as if she had just let go of a heavy burden.

"Hello!" came a loud voice. It was a child's voice and I realized it was coming from the spirit who was going to take the body Patti was creating. I very clearly saw a little boy right next to his mother. Patti was at that time hoping for and expecting a little girl, but from this hello, there was no doubt in my mind that her baby was a boy. I sent a non-verbal hello back to him and watched his energy and his mother's both glow in response. They were ready!

As the reading progressed, Patti looked more and more at ease and started to laugh and enjoy herself. Halfway through, she said

"My contractions have started!" But she was not concerned and so we continued happily.

By the end of the reading, she was glowing and smiling and enjoying her contractions; so she went her way and I went mine, very excited about the tremendous reading I had done.

On Monday morning, I went into the Church Office as usual and within the hour, Patti arrived with her two sisters and her new baby. "I wanted to come by and thank you," she said. "That was a wonderful reading on Friday night, and a great way to begin giving birth! My sisters came over when I got home and I was only in labor for five hours!"

She drew back the blanket and held her baby out for me to see. "Sue, I want you to meet my son, Eric!" As I looked at Eric, I saw the same bright spirit I had seen on Friday night, and we exchanged our second hellos.

Rev. Sue Pearce

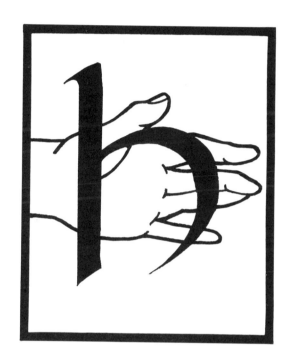

healing

Medical invalidation (you are not in charge of your body, the doctor is) has caused many people to find the doorstep of the Berkeley Psychic Institute. What has attracted people to psychic healing is its simplicity and that it works. You are the creator of your own healing miracle.

1   TELLING THE TRUTH FROM THE LIE

first came to the Berkeley Psychic Institute on a lark, but also because part of me was desperate. Although I had multiple health problems, I had learned to live with most of them with the daily help of about eight aspirin, two or three antihistamines and an allergy injection.

It was the BIGGIE that I was frightened about: I had a brain tumor that rested on my pituitary gland.

As time went by, it caused an alarming increase in the level of prolactin in my body (a hormone produced by the pituitary gland). This in turn caused other symptoms—chronic lactation (breast milk), frequent headaches, a weight gain of 100 pounds in less than a year, and irregular menstrual cycles. "This tumor will force you into an early menopause," the doctors told me. "It will soon interfere with your vision; and eventually it will probably kill you."

Doctors. Oh yes, I had doctors! I had an internist, an endocrinologist, an ophthalmologist, a neurologist, a neuro-surgeon, a gynecologist and an allergist. And I was a registered nurse who worked for an internist, and most of my friends and relatives were in some area of the medical field. Surrounded!

The doctors recommended surgery. They offered to cut up into my nose, drill through my sinuses and carve the tumor out of my brain. I said, "Wait," and I went to the Berkeley Psychic Institute.

I had a healing. WOW, what was that? I felt something. I had a reading. I was fascinated. But life went on and I didn't have time for any classes. Another blood test; the prolactin was even higher. "If it reaches 200," warned the doctors, "you're having surgery." (Normal level is 20.) The Berkeley Psychic Institute people offered to have some students and a teacher work with me on a regular basis for a while. My friends and colleagues said "Surgery!"

I went to the BPI for one-hour weekly healing sessions for two months. They said hello to me. They showed me how to ground. They laughed a lot. Pretty soon, I laughed a lot and things began happening. The blood test results began to fall. I went to my allergist and stopped the medications, then got retested. The allergies were gone! We hadn't even been working on the allergies!

I enrolled in the Beginning Healing Class, still continuing to see my doctor. More tests, and the doctors were confused. Tumors don't recede!

Then came the lie. The neurosurgeon informed me that my latest X-rays showed a worsening of the tumor. "We must operate at once," he said. "You must get that thing removed before it's too late." And, not realizing where I worked, he told a different story in a letter to my boss, relating how much better-looking my latest X-rays were, and saying that he was going to get in there fast to get a piece of that tumor before it was all gone; he wanted to study it for his research. After all, tumors aren't supposed to disappear! I saw the letter, cancelled my surgery and returned to Beginning Healing Class.

Now, after nearly four years of healing myself on a regular basis, all that is left is a lot of the weight that I had gained. My prolactin blood levels are normal; my menstrual cycle is normal; the headaches are gone.

And oh, yes, I've left my body to science when I die. I don't mind their trying to analyze what happened, but not at my expense. They can wait for my body until I'm finished with it!

Rev. Helen Rose Carr

WHOSE HAND IS IT, ANYWAY?

 friend of mine, Joseph, had an accident in which a machine went out of control and trapped his hand beneath the handle. His family told me he was seriously hurt and they encouraged me to visit him at the hospital because they thought I might cheer him up.

So I went to visit him. His hand and arm were wrapped in gauze with just the fingertips sticking out. They were black—not black and blue, just black and dead-looking. I was about to ask him if he'd like a healing but for some reason, I decided to wait.

Ten minutes later I knew why. First, the surgeon came in who was to operate on him in the morning. "Well, Joseph," he said jovially, "I've studied your X-rays and I think it's only your middle three fingers that are going to have to come off." After a few more minutes of conversation he left and some nurses dropped by to exclaim and commiserate. "Look at those fingers! Talk about necrotic! Wow, you poor guy—losing three fingers at your age! He reminds me of that motorcycle accident we had in here last month . . ." Then Joseph's mother called from Indiana and fortunately I couldn't hear her, but I could tell from watching Joseph that she wasn't exactly cheering him up.

I sat there, amused, as I waited for three and a half hours to ask Joseph if he would like a healing. After the phone call, I finally asked him. "Yes, please!" he gasped. I got him out of bed and into a chair. I put a huge protection rose up at the door to stop anyone else from coming in.

As I sat across from him, I went into a light trance. I grounded him and started draining all the medical attention from his body. "Know what, old man?" I said.

"What?"

"You're not running any energy in your injured arm. When that doctor told you that you'd have to lose those fingers, you immediately disowned them. Now I'm going to start your energy running there again, and when you can feel it, tell me."

After about 45 minutes, his eyes opened wide and he exclaimed, "I can feel it, Ed! I can feel it! My arm is tingling as if it had fallen asleep! What are you doing?"

"Well, is it your hand or isn't it! I'm running your own energy down and out your fingertips. Now I'm going to have my healing guide move out the drug energy that's in your system. That will help your own immune system to function."

I finished the healing by filling him up with neutral gold energy that would help him to own his space, and helped him back into bed.

"And remember," I said, as I left him for the night, "own that arm! When they wheel you off to surgery tomorrow, be sure you run your energy all the way down and out your fingers. You can create anything you want to! You know that don't you?"

"Yeah," he cheered hopefully.

The next night, I called him at the hospital.

"Ed!" he shouted. "Guess what! They only took off a little piece of one finger! I owned my arm and hand like you said! I ran my energy through it, and I still have four and a half fingers!"

"Good job!" I said.

"So give your healing guide a pat on the back. And yourself too. Not a bad team!"

Since I had had my healing guide for only two weeks, this was very validating. And I got to look at how the medical profession invalidates our ability to heal ourselves and how spirit really does heal the body.

Rev. Ed Mosur

TWIN TUMOR

1 was visiting at my parents' house when my older brother, Ned, and his wife, Janine, were visiting too. On the second day, Ned woke up feeling nauseated, headachy and frightened. He wouldn't get out of bed even when my mother coaxed him with his favorite breakfast of pancakes and bacon.

After breakfast, I sat down to run my energy and took a clairvoyant look at his space. I saw the shape of a tumor in his head. I watched it for a bit and then got up and went into his room. "Ned," I said to the hump under the blankets, "Did one of your friends die recently?"

"Yes," he mumbled.

"Of a tumor behind the eye?"

A hand reached out and pulled the covers away from two squinting brown eyes. "Yes," he said. "How did you know?"

"I looked at you," I answered, grinning at his puzzlement.

"That was Robert!" exclaimed his wife who was sitting by his bed. "He died just last month. Ned was upset about it."

"Yes. You're matching him," I said. "You've put an energy tumor in your own head to match his."

Silence.

"That spot on your eye!" said Janine. "Just last night," she explained to me, "Ned was saying that there's this spot on his eye that won't go away and he's afraid it's a tumor."

"What a creative guy," I said. "He not only builds houses, he builds tumors too!"

"Shut up, kid," muttered Ned.

"Want me to get rid of it for you?" I offered.

"Sure."

I grounded him, gathered up the tumor energy into some roses out in front of him and exploded them. Then I filled the space up with his own gold-orange healing energy and left him to snooze.

That evening he ate his usual giant dinner and beat me at poker again. I don't know why I'm so nice to him.

A Healing Student

THE DAY I BECAME A HEALER

1 had just joined the Clairvoyant Training Program of the Berkeley Psychic Institute and one of my favorite things to do was to go to the Healing Clinics on Monday evenings and do healings. I was very excited about learning to use my healing abilities and I never knew who might walk in the door and what new experience I might have.

Rev. John Luby was the healing teacher in Santa Rosa at that time and he ran the Healing Clinic, saying hello to everyone and helping the beginners like me to gain confidence in using their tools.

One evening, after I had done a couple of healings and was feeling happy with my increased certainty, John asked me to give a healing to a woman named Kristi who looked very pale and drained.

"Hello," I said to her. "Would you like a healing?"

"Yes please," she said. As I began to ground her and find the edge of her aura, she said, "I have a physical problem. I began hemorrhaging three days ago and it's getting worse. I'm wondering if I'm going to need an operation . . ."

*Well, so much for my new certainty! I immediately thought
that there was nothing I could do about a problem as serious as
this, and I felt afraid and out of my league. So I went and got
John, knowing that he was the only person experienced enough
to do this healing. He looked at Kristi clairvoyantly for a moment
and said, "There's a spirit who would like to have a body, who is
plugged into the female baby-making machinery of Kristi's
body."*

Great! I thought. Now he'll take that spirit out.

*"Why don't you go ahead and move that spirit out for her,
Shelley?" John said, and stood back to watch me.*

*Well, I stood there in shock, so sure that I couldn't do it—and
yet seeing how I would do it if I could. John was waiting. Kristi
was waiting. In my fog of fear and uncertainty, I made a decision.
I would move that spirit out as if I knew how. So I went ahead
and when I was finished, Kristi thanked me and left.*

*"Good job," said John. But what about her bleeding? I
wondered.*

*At a Healing Clinic a few weeks later, a woman came up to me
and said, "Kristi asked me to thank you. She said her bleeding
stopped that evening after you gave her a healing and she's been
fine ever since. She wanted me to be sure to let you know."*

*Well, that was the validation I needed in order to let go of my
uncertainty. Not only could I see what to do, but I could do it
and it worked! I accepted myself as a healer that day and have
been creating miracles ever since!*

Rev. Shelley Hodgen

MAKING CHANGES

O ne evening a woman named Barbara came into
the Berkeley Psychic Institute of Santa Rosa for a
*reading. One of the things she was interested in was getting some
information about her boyfriend, Ernie, who was dying of cancer. So during her reading, we gave a long-distance reading and
healing to Ernie.*

As the center chair reader, I started out by saying hello to him as a spirit and asking him to show me what was happening to him. From the pictures that danced across my reading screen, I saw that his ex-wife was in a legal battle with him for money and would not let him see his children; that his insurance business was about to go bankrupt; and that Barbara was totally smothering his space in her attempts to heal him. I saw that he had created leaving his body because he did not know any other way to make some space for himself away from his family and problems.

As a spirit, I taught him about grounding and getting tough in his own space, and told him that he could tell the people in his space to get out—he didn't have to be the one to leave his body!

As he became aware that it was these other people's energy that he was trying to get away from by dying, he became very angry; then as he started to practice what I had taught him, he laughed, it was so simple. All he had to do was recognize them, say hello to them spirit-to-spirit and ask them to leave.

He asked me to help him further in healing his body. So I psychically took one of his cells, cleaned it out and put in the postulate that it was a very healthy cell and that the other cells would follow suit. In trance I saw him accept that cell into his body and start the healing process.

We finished Barbara's reading and she left.

• • • • •

Three years went by and we saw nothing more of her. Then one day, I ran into her again in the grocery store and she reminded me of the reading. I asked her what had happened to Ernie. In some disgust, she told me that soon after her reading, he had broken up with her, sold his insurance business, broken off connections with his ex-wife, and his cancer had gone into total remission. The last she had heard of him was that he seemed to be miraculously cured of his cancer and had married someone else. He had become a pilot and was flying back and forth to Hawaii with a charter business he had begun.

I stood in the store listening in delight and amazement to this update. Ernie had created an entirely new and happier life for himself. He had healed himself after simply receiving the spiritual information that he could have and own his own space.

What a capable spirit!

Rev. Cathy Langlois

1 NOW YOU SEE IT, NOW YOU DON'T!

was working in the Women's Healing Center in San Rafael when Rene, one of the graduates of the Berkeley Psychic Institute, called for some help and communication. She had been sick with fever, abdominal pains and general flu-like symptoms. Her doctor had initially diagnosed it as a virus but when Rene had returned to her a week later presenting the same symptoms, she had found a fibrous tumor the size of an orange on Rene's right ovary. The doctor had urged her to go for exploratory surgery the following Monday (this was on Wednesday), at which time, if the surgeons found things to be bad, they would perform a complete hysterectomy.

I invited her to come in for a healing at the Clinic that evening. First, I had my healing guides work throughout her aura and body, moving out energy which was not in affinity with her. Then they worked on her womb, ovaries and the entire network of female energy connections. Then I asked her to sit in on the reading line for the rest of the evening, so she could continue to run her energy and heal herself.

Towards the end of the evening, I put her in the "hot seat" and asked the line to look at her. What they saw was a baby being attached to her right ovary by an energy cord. They also saw competition energy (who could heal this body better—the family, the doctors or Rene?) and "prove-it" energy: ("If you're a psychic healer, let's see if you can heal yourself!") So the readers began to look at what caused her to be affected by all this energy and they saw that this was one of the ways she was learning about a female body and how to heal it.

They described to Rene how her own healing energy had been covered up by all the foreign energy; then they moved it out and filled her up with her own healing energy.

On Friday she called to tell us that after her pre-surgical tests the doctors could find no tumor. It was completely gone!

Rev. Jan Classen

"I WISH I WAS A BETTER HEALER!"

My daughter Jenny had been sick for over a week with what I saw clairvoyantly as appendicitis. I had been working on healing her but, unable to effect a cure and feeling invalidated because I hadn't succeeded, I took her to the hospital. They checked her out and said, "It's probably not appendicitis, because that's very rare in three-year-olds. It's just a touch of the flu."

I took her home, but she got no better. I took her to the hospital again. This time the doctors diagnosed a ruptured appendix. They said it had ruptured more than eight hours earlier! They were extremely worried. I saw their worry and their concern not only for Jenny, but for me, the grieving mother! But I wasn't grieving or even concerned, even though I was being given large doses of sympathy. Instead I felt validated, confident. I tried to become sad and worried because it seemed that as the mother I was supposed to act this way. I decided to meditate in a private waiting room.

During the operation, I felt in touch with her and since she was now in no pain, I relaxed even more and sent her a hello, a healing and a pat on the back.

An hour later, the doctors came out, relieved and shaking their heads in perplexity. "It was the strangest and luckiest thing," they said. "Never seen anything like it before." They had found Jenny's appendix to be healed and closed. The infection that had escaped had been held in place by her intestines which had moved to form a barrier.

They still worried, though. "She'll have to stay here for three weeks," they said. "She must be monitored closely."

Jenny had other ideas. She rebelled against the shots, drugs and tubes, and broke one machine after another with her Yin Yang* energy. One night, when four nurses were holding her down for two doctors to try and examine her, she yelled out loudly, "Mommy, I wish I was a better healer!"

Silence. Everyone stood still. I broke down and cried. Out came the tubes; nurses stopped drawing blood. Machines were wheeled out of the room. The doctor reduced her medication.

One week after her admission, Jenny left the hospital, healed.

Rev. Jeanette Gurling White

Jenny had learned her healing skills at The Yin Yang Seminary for Psychic Children of the Church of Divine Man. See General Introduction.

I'M PRETTY

A t a Psychic Fair in San Francisco, a teenager came to the Healing Booth where I was working and asked for a healing. Her shoulders were hunched and her face deformed; she drooled and her speech was garbled.

"I wonder if there is anything you can do to help me," she said with some difficulty. "I have a brain tumor and it will be operated on in the morning."

I sat down opposite her and went into trance. I said hello to her as spirit. The first thing I noticed was another being in her space. It was a relative who had died within the last couple of years and, instead of taking its next step, had moved into her space. With her permission I removed this being and sent it on its way.

Immediately her facial features regained balance.

Then I worked on her brain cells, reversing the damage done by the presence of that being, and filled them up with her own golden healing energy. Finally, I worked on the connection between her and her body, removing energy which invalidated her ability to heal herself.

After about forty-five minutes I was done and I opened my eyes. She had stopped drooling and her back was straighter. "Thank you very much," she said, as clear as a bell, and went on her way.

Three weeks later, I got a phone call from her. The doctors had removed a tumor the size of an orange and were incredulous both at how easy it had been and at her rate of recovery. She had been out of bed four hours after the anesthesia had worn off. The man in the next room had had the identical operation for a tumor the size of a cherry and was still comatose when she was discharged.

"It was your healing that made the difference," she said. "I want to thank you. I can walk normally now and I even think I'm pretty!"

Rt. Rev. Michael J Tamura

A GREAT (DANE) HEALING

While I was taking the Beginning Healing Class, I was caretaker at a friend's house in San Anselmo. One of the animals I was caring for was an elderly Great Dane whose stiff back legs made it difficult for her to walk. She also had a urinary problem that caused her to cry out whenever she urinated.

One day I was digging near one of her favorite sitting spots in the fenced acre of land. She hobbled up and eased herself into a position to watch me. After I had worked there for an hour or two, I started back down the hill and called for her to follow. She tried to stand up but sank back down, looking very pitiful.

The idea flashed through my head: "I am a healer! If I can do healings on people why can't I heal this dog?" Using the techniques I had learned at the Berkeley Psychic Institute I gave her a healing right there. I knew when she had had enough because she suddenly stood up and galloped back and forth across the yard three times! When she squatted down to urinate she was quiet and even seemed to be smiling. Then she trotted over to me as if to say "OK, I'm ready to go down the hill now."

I remember thinking, "Wow, I don't think she's kidding me!"

Rev. Kathy Kwiatkowski

INSTANT HEART REPAIR

Karen came into the Berkeley Psychic Institute of Santa Rosa asking for a long-distance healing for her father, who had had a heart attack and was in the hospital.

I asked her to sit down in front of me and relax. I grounded myself and went into a light trance. "Could you say your father's name a couple of times for me?" I asked. "It will help me make spiritual contact with him."

"Frank McKinnon," she said, and I could hear the grief and worry in her voice.

"That's great," I said. "I see your father now. I'm going to take a few minutes to talk to him on a spirit-to-spirit level, and see what this business with his heart is all about." I said hello to Frank. He seemed surprised to be receiving this type of communication. Apparently not many people had ever recognized or communicated to him as spirit. I explained to him who I was and what was happening and asked if he would like a healing. He said yes.

Clairvoyantly I could see the damage that had occurred in his heart. I asked my healing guide to repair the torn tissue in his left atrium. As he worked, I described what I saw to Karen. When the torn tissue was repaired and the area was filled with Frank's own orange healing energy, I said goodbye to him and separated from my healing guide.

"That was a good healing," I told Karen, and she left feeling much better than when she had arrived.

● ● ● ● ●

About a month later, at a party, I met a man who was a friend of Karen's.

"Remember that long-distance healing you did on her father?" he asked.

"Yes," I replied. "How did he do?"

"It was incredible! The very next day his heart was better. The doctors said that it seemed to have repaired itself. They couldn't understand it. They said it was a miracle!"

Rev. Sharon Santos

A FEMALE HEALING

When I first came to the Berkeley Psychic Institute I had recurrent bladder and kidney problems. The bladder infections I learned to endure. As a nurse-midwife I just carried antibiotics with me everywhere and at the first sign of a bladder infection I took a one-time "double the dose" amount. In this way I could stop the infection and avoid a ten-day course of medicine. I thought this solution very clever. I also drank huge amounts of herbal teas and took herbal remedies so the symptoms wouldn't occur as frequently.

The kidney infections were a different story. They caused fevers, backache and blood in the urine. I was told I needed an IVP—an X-ray test with dye shot through the kidneys. I knew that if I had this test I'd be worse so I refused, much to the concern of my fellow medical workers.

While I was in the Clairvoyant Training Program I heard the Very Rt. Rev. Lewis Bostwick tell the story about his wife, Susan, and the bladder problems she had had before joining the Berkeley Psychic Institute. After hearing this story I went to the next event Susan taught, a Female Retreat. At the Retreat I approached her and asked for some help. She sat me down and looked clairvoyantly at my problem. She communicated that she saw male energy—some of it was my father's love—stuck in my abdomen. She removed the male energy and then gave me a female healing guide. This guide was to work only on my bladder and kidneys. I was to work with this guide on a daily basis for five to ten minutes.

Needless to say, I was very skeptical but I didn't have anything to lose so I began to do as instructed. The results were astounding! Whenever I felt my bladder or kidney problem starting I'd call in my healing guide and within a few minutes I'd be back to normal.

Within the past seven years I've only had one infection; I'd say that was truly a miracle!

Rev. Carol Tracy Cullinen

BY-PASSING DEATH

a friend of mine, Jerry, was scheduled for a double by-pass heart surgery from which the doctors predicted a fifty/fifty chance of recovery. (He'd already had two heart attacks by age forty-two.) A few hours after the long, involved surgery he began to develop "serious complications" and was returned to the operating room to have the surgery redone. It was during this time that I called his wife, Sherry, to see how he was doing. When she told me what was happening I asked her if she would like me to arrange a long-distance healing. She said "Sure, anything you can do would be great!"

I called the Berkeley Psychic Institute and explained the situation. They said to come in. The timing was perfect. There was a Psychic Abilities Demonstration going on just then so there were three or four students from the Clairvoyant Training Program and two staff members. They had me sit in front of a line of readers so as to become a channel connecting them more clearly with Jerry's energy. They found him hovering several feet above his body, very concerned and confused about what was happening. As they worked, they saw the doctors discussing his condition, saying that they didn't believe he would survive this second surgery and that it was futile to even try to save him. One of the nurses in the room was directing very negative energy toward him. For some reason she didn't want him to survive. There were two other nurses in the room, who were healers and helping as much as possible. The readers communicated to Jerry as a spirit, asking him if he was ready to leave his body for this lifetime. He said no, he still had some things he wanted to do, but was confused and didn't know how to get back into his body—could they help?

The readers grounded the operating room, the doctors, the nurses, and Jerry's body, and proceeded to clear out all the nurses' and doctors' energy from his space. They also cleaned out the extremely high level of drug energy in his body. Then they connected him up to his own healing energy and survival information and placed a "Maria" (a protective spirit guide) above him to keep away any foreign energy that might interfere with his own healing process during the next few days.

Well, Jerry not only survived, but regained his health and strength more and more as the months rolled by. He said he felt *"really great." Many of his friends and family said "Thank God; it was a miracle, a blessing. . . ."*

Rev. Sabina Krumpe

A DOG'S LIFE

Mrs. Peterson brought in her cocker spaniel, Muffie, for treatment. Muffie had been to several other veterinarians for flea allergy dermatitis. His back was losing hair and the skin was red and raw. He would scratch himself until he bled; scabs would form and he would scratch them open. The medication Mrs. Peterson had received for him from the other vets worked only for short periods of time and as soon as it was discontinued, the problem returned.

I made a quick examination of Muffie and then asked Mrs. Peterson to leave him in the treatment room and join me in my office.

"What can be done?" she moaned, twisting her well-manicured hands. "I'm so worried about him! I feel itchy myself when he carries on like that!"

I hid a smile. "Are you telling me, Mrs. Peterson, that you have Muffie's problem too?"

"Fleas!" she cried, smoothing her skirt. "Most certainly not! How can you . . ." She caught my smile. "Oh, you don't mean that, doctor!"

I sat her down. "Mrs. Peterson, the fleas are not the problem."

"Oh! You mean the allergy . . . ?"

"No. The allergy isn't the problem either."

"I don't know what you mean."

I wondered how much I could explain to this lady. "Mrs. Peterson, your concern is the problem."

She sat still, trying to figure out whether I was insulting her or joking.

"The energy of your concern is getting into Muffie's space so he can't heal himself. I understand your anxiety, and it's natural, but you need to keep it in your own space. May I give you both a quick healing on an energy level? It might help you to see my meaning."

She gave a dazed nod, her mind clearly going a hundred miles a minute.

I grounded her and Muffie, and called back her energy from Muffie, forming it into a gold sun over her head. I asked her Akashic Record Keeper to give her some of her own information about making separations, and I put that in the gold sun too. I brought the gold sun down into her space and I filled Muffie with his own healing energy.

"You can call your energy back any time," I said, "from Muffie or anyone else. Just imagine a gold sun above your head which is a magnet and will attract your energy back to you." As I spoke, she did it.

"Good job!" I said. "Let's go back to Muffie." We went back into the treatment room. Muffie was lying still under the table, chin resting on his paws. He ran out, tail wagging, as we entered and I picked him up and examined his skin. It was normal. No redness and no attempts to scratch.

Mrs. Peterson started fondling and talking to him and within a couple of minutes, he was scratching again. "Got a gold sun up there?" I asked with a grin. She heard me and pulled her energy back into her own space. Muffie stopped scratching.

About a month later, I examined Muffie. His skin was normal and his hair was growing back again.

Rev. Steve Drlica, D.V.M.

PLEASE HELP!

lease! You've got to help me!"

I was handling some paperwork in my office when those words reached my ears. From their tone, I knew I'd better get out to the reception area.

A man was leaning over the receptionist, the energy of desperation surrounding him.

"Hello," I said. "I'm Michael Tamura, the Director here. Can I help you?"

"I hope so. I don't know where else to turn!"

I invited him into the sitting room and listened to his story. He was here because of his wife, Jean, who had been in a serious accident about a month before. Her car had rolled down an embankment. She was now paralyzed from the neck down with severe damage to her back and all the doctors could do was help her psyche, to try to brighten her mental outlook.

"I even went on national TV and asked for people's prayers but nothing has happened. This is my last resort. Do you think you can help?"

I explained that we were a Church and believed in communication of spirit. I told him I'd take a look at the situation and we would go from there.

I had three other psychics form a reading line across from Frank. I stood next to him, resting one of my hands on the back of his neck and with the other, lightly touching the center of his forehead.

"Frank, I want you to form a mental image picture of Jean. Picture her in perfect health, happy and laughing. This will help us make a psychic connection with her."

Once Frank got the picture of Jean firmly established in his head, I walked around in front of him and took my place in the reading line. It took about thirty minutes to get through the white prayer energy that had been generated by his national TV plea for help. When I could finally see Jean clairvoyantly, I noticed how very angry she was as a being.

Using my clairvoyant ability, I saw what had happened and told Frank about it.

"I see Jean wasn't alone in the car when the accident happened. It looks as if her mother, aunt and sister were with her. There's also a young boy—is it your son?"

Frank confirmed the scene I was seeing on my psychic reading screen. I continued talking to Frank while I clairaudiently communicated with Jean. With her permission I did some healing. I did what is known as an out-of-body healing. As a spirit, I left my body and entered Jean's body through the back of her head. From there I removed all of the destruction energy and the people who were stopping her from healing herself. I also worked on the programming from the doctors that said she would be paralyzed for life.

I worked on the spinal damage and on her energy channels and pain. I finished by returning to my body and filling Jean up with a golden healing energy.

A few days later Frank called, very excited.

"Michael, she can move both of her arms now. It's a miracle! Can you do some more work on her?"

The following Thursday the four of us, who had worked on Jean previously, went to the hospital for our first "on-site" visit and healing. We talked to her for about an hour and I again did an out-of-body healing. This time I cleaned out her nerves and tissues, re-attached the broken circuits and worked on the pain. On a spirit level I did some teaching, showing Jean how she could work on herself and have seniority over the doctors. I also gave her a psychic surgeon who would continue to help her.

When the healing was finished we said our goodbyes and left. The following Monday Frank again called.

"Michael, I'll never be able to thank you enough. Jean now has full use of her fingers! Can you continue healing her?"

On Wednesday we again went to the hospital. After a while we put Jean in a wheelchair and took her out into an open court. The fresh air and sunshine were good for her and outside of the hospital building we had more permission to work with her. We talked for about an hour about all kinds of things—about her job as an electrician and what was happening to her in her everyday environment. We gave her a clairvoyant reading and finally I again did an out-of-body healing. This time I worked on a cellular level, removing any damage and programming her cells to be healthy. I removed more of the medical invalidation and generally "cleaned house."

A few days later Frank called with an update on Jean's condition. She now had complete sensation all the way down to her feet.

The next week we arrived at the hospital as usual. When we rounded the nurses' station on our way to Jean's room, one of the nurses stopped us.

"I'm sorry but no one is allowed to see Jean except her doctor and husband."

"I'm Jean's minister."

"I'm sorry, I mean no one at all except her doctor and husband."

After a few more questions the nurse said that Jean was in extensive therapy from morning until night, using a walking bar, and was strictly regimented.

I still wanted to see her anyway, so we went to her room, only to find that they had moved her.

We never saw Jean or heard from Frank again.

Rt. Rev. Michael J Tamura

SHALL WE DANCE?

I had an injured ankle that caused me to limp. When I went to the doctor he gave me a foot brace and told me to wear it. The foot brace was supposed to help heal my ankle. When this didn't help he gave me cortisone shots. After several weeks' worth of treatment I still limped.

I went to see a second doctor who told me I limped because I had corns, so he removed my corns. I still limped.

Finally, I asked two Berkeley Psychic Institute teachers to look clairvoyantly at my foot. Reverends Richard Lawrence and Cecelia Bailey saw a past life picture that was located in my knee and ankle; this was what was causing the pain. They removed the picture and did some psychic healing work. This took place on a Thursday and on the following Sunday I was dancing!

Rev. Veronica Griffith

BACK ON HIS FEET

I had just received my healing guide in a beginning Healing Class at the Berkeley Psychic Institute. The next day I went to work at the hospital where I am a respiratory therapist. One of my patients that day was an old priest who was in his eighties and was in a coma in Intensive Care. He had not opened his eyes or spoken for at least a month.

I went in to give him a respiratory treatment and, keeping an eye out for the nurse, began giving him a healing with my new healing guide. I started at the crown chakra, then the sixth, and as I was moving down to the fifth chakra, his eyes popped open and he said "Who are you?"

"My name is Barbara. I am your respiratory therapist and I'm giving you a breathing treatment."

He seemed to accept this and I continued giving him the healing. When the respiratory treatment was over I left the room.

Later I was walking by his room and heard two nurses talking as they were making his bed. "Father, you look so much better!" said one. "Doesn't he, Jan! Look at the color in his face!" The priest was conscious, but he was still a bit confused and he just laughed and said, "You girls do such wonderful work."

I watched and was validated every day as I saw him get back on his feet. I didn't tell anyone in the hospital that I had given him a healing; I just smiled to myself every time I saw him.

Finally, after a few weeks he could walk on his own and was not confused or disoriented. One could not tell that he had ever been in a coma at all. He left the hospital with plans to take a trip to Ireland to visit his family.

Rev. Barbara Keck

BOUNCING HIM BACK

Bobby had been bounced off the bed by his older brothers and had landed on his head, suffering a concussion. After a whole day, he was still unconscious or nearly so and had vomited all of what little food he had taken.

Distraught with worry, his mother, Jan, brought him into the Healing Clinic in San Jose. He was pale, limp, clammy-skinned and apparently unaware of his surroundings. When I looked at him clairvoyantly, I could see him hovering about three feet over his body.

The healing teacher, Thelma Meites, and I were to give them both healings. Little did I know as I sat down to practice my psychic skills that I was being given an opportunity by the healing teacher to experience my first miracle. I was a beginner and only later realized what happened when Thelma moved aside and "put me to work."

I worked on Jan; I grounded her and drew her aura closer to her body so she could start to feel less frightened and get back in touch with her own information on how to cope. I also grounded her fear out of Bobby's body. Thelma was working on Bobby; each time she grounded him, he twitched all over and started making sucking motions. Jan then began to relax, and gave him diluted apple juice. He kept it down.

At this point Thelma turned over to me the healing of Bobby and asked me to work from a light trance state. She stepped aside to observe my work. I noticed that Bobby had moved closer—to about 18 inches above his body. He looked perplexed, slightly amused and not at all worried. However, his body was still limp and vibrating at a low energy level, mostly because of his long absence and the concussion on his crown.

I looked at the communication space between him and his body. There was a slender, sky-blue cord between him and his heart chakra. (Thelma confirmed that she had hooked him up to the God of his Heart). The main problem seemed to be some very dark energy in the area of the concussion. It consisted mostly of one brother's worry energy and death pictures from the whole family. I read what the dark energy said: "This body is probably going to die." No wonder Bobby wasn't getting back in!

I grounded off that dark, foreign energy and helped Bobby replace it with his own healing energy—a nice orange tinged with brown. Now he moved in very close to his head. I asked him as spirit what he needed in order to come all the way into his body; his answer was that he wanted to regain the information on how he got bounced out of his body and how to get back in. I looked for that information and found it in the Akashic Records right above his head and the crown chakra. So I connected it with a light cord of energy to his first chakra at the base of the spine.

That was all it took. He immediately slid back into his body. A whimpering sound told me to come out of trance and open my eyes and there he was, wide awake, alert and moving! He reached for Jan and in a few moments was holding his own bottle and drinking heartily.

I laughed in amazement at his vitality and his mother's relief. How gratifying to see such immediate and spectacular results; yet all Thelma and I had done really, was to clean out the *communication space between two beings, their bodies, their information and the planet.*

Rev. Caitlin Goodsell

NO SURGERY, THANKS

1 had a pap smear that came back "class three": I had irregular cells in my cervix, which could be cancerous. The proper name for this is "severe dysplasia." After a time I began to call it severe displeasure.

When I returned to my doctor, he immediately wanted to call the hospital to admit me and cut out part of my cervix. Being unprepared and somewhat frightened, I agreed to be admitted the next week.

Meanwhile, I told Rev. Richard Lawrence at the Berkeley Psychic Institute what was happening. He had someone take a look at me clairvoyantly on a female level and communicate what was happening to my body. With the reader's help I began to heal myself. First I cleared out all the black energy in my reproductive system. This was the first time I had clairvoyantly looked at my female creative energy and my reproductive system. Wow! There was a lot going on and I didn't own too much of it for myself.

Now it was time to get back to my doctor and tell him the news. No way was I going to the hospital! Well, he was angry, very angry, but we did manage to make an agreement. I would be back in three months to have another pap smear.

During those three months I ran my healing energy and created the postulate that my cervix had only healthy cells. I began by putting a drop of gold healing energy on each ovary and having that gold increase and spread throughout my reproductive system. I also continued to drain out all foreign energy down my grounding cord.

Back to the doctor. I didn't go to the hospital and the final pap smear after the biopsy was negative. A miracle!

Rev. Linda Enos

WHAT'S IN A CAT SCAN?

Jimmy was a small, curly-haired boy of about six, who had a tumor behind his eye. His mother had taken him to the Stanford Medical Clinic for diagnosis and treatment. The doctors there told her that Jimmy would lose his eye, but they explained that it wasn't all bad; Jimmy could have a glass eye for cosmetic purposes.

Jimmy's mother, Marilyn, brought him to the Healing Clinic held at the Berkeley Psychic Institute of San Jose on three separate occasions. She would usually come by on the way to or coming back from Stanford. It was really hard on her to bring him in because she was fighting the energy of Stanford—scientific atheism versus spiritual communication and healing. Stanford had Marilyn convinced that Jimmy would die if she didn't have him operated on yesterday. Obviously, she felt very guilty.

Rev. John Fulton directed the healing sessions with Jimmy and the two of them developed a special rapport. The healers in the Healing Clinic worked on the energy in Jimmy's head, but more importantly, instilled certainty in him that he could own his space. By the third visit, Jimmy had reclaimed much of his certainty and space back and we, the healers, clairvoyantly saw that he had completely removed the energy causing the tumor.

Marilyn took Jimmy back for a CAT scan and the results showed that the tumor had completely disappeared! The doctors, however, told her that this second CAT scan was probably a mistake, that the first one was accurate and Jimmy needed the operation right away.

We did not hear from Marilyn or Jimmy after that, but I validated and consoled myself that Jimmy was a very capable young man, who had already created one miracle, and that he now had the tools to create whatever he wanted.

This healing taught me about guilty mothers, past life agreements, a spirit's ability to create change and have it all, and how good the medical profession is at invalidating our ability to heal ourselves.

Rev. Mary Miller Fulton

RAPID HEALING

Julie and I were floating down the river on two big rubber tubes. It was a great day: a good combination of exciting rapids and a relaxing float. We had been in the water for three hours and had about one hour left to go. As it was starting to get a little cold and windy, Julie wanted to stop.

"How about hitching a ride down to the parking lot, Jon?" she asked. At that moment, we hit a big set of rapids. I grabbed on to my tube, bouncing and jolting along with spray in my face and the sound of crashing water in my ears. I heard Julie scream behind me. As soon as I could, I looked over my shoulder and saw that she had fallen off her tube and was being thrown from rock to rock by the force of the white water.

My tube got stuck for a moment against a large rock so I climbed out onto it. As the water tossed Julie past my rock, I leaned down, grabbed her arm and managed to pull her out. She was as limp as a rag doll, breathing heavily and her thighs were streaming blood. I leaned her carefully against the sun-warmed rock. "Sit back, Julie," I said. "Just get your breath. You have a big gash down each side of your pelvis. Would you like me to give you a healing?"

She nodded. I was nervous because both of her cuts were at least two inches long and about a quarter of an inch open, and were bleeding heavily. It looked as if she would need stitches, but since we weren't close to any help, I knew it was up to me. I could also see that she was in a lot of pain.

Without going into trance, I used my clairaudient abilities to talk to my healing guides and asked them to help. They were excited to work on this so I just let them go, while I watched and passed on to Julie what they were telling me.

The first thing they did was to take out all of her resistance to the pain, because it was holding the pain in her body. Next they drained out everyone else's energy from the injured parts of her body. This gave her enough room to heal herself. As she brought in her own orange-colored healing energy, things began to happen. Within two or three minutes, the gash on the left side of her pelvis had completely closed so that you could barely tell it had been there. The gash on the right side stopped bleeding entirely and began to close also.

We sat on that warm rock in the wind and laughed in delight at our healing abilities. By the time we got home that night, you couldn't even tell that she had been injured.

Rev. Jon Cotton

HEALING ASTHMA

y eleven-year-old son Jonathan was living with his father. One day he called me at work. He was having trouble breathing and was wheezing badly. "Mom, I don't feel very good. Dad told me to stay home today because I vomited all over the place." His voice was forlorn and I felt bad for him. I talked to him a little more, guided him through breathing exercises but knew when I hung up the phone that he was still not feeling very well. I decided to go over and see him.

Jonathan and I had talked a lot about what I was learning at the Berkeley Psychic Institute. He knew that naturally he was a healthy and happy boy and that only when energy that wasn't his got into his space did he feel bad.

I pulled my car into the driveway of my ex-husband's house and took a moment to find my space. I grounded, moved out as much of the concern for Jonathan as I could, and brought in lots of amusement. Using roses, I cleaned out the communication space between me and the God of my Heart and then proceeded into the house.

Jonathan was lying in his bed; when he saw me he started to cry and choked out: "Mommy, I don't feel good!" At this point I was very glad that I had taken those few moments in the driveway to find my space; I was able to keep from matching his pain and confusion. I gave him a kiss and a hug and a big smile. "Jonathan, you want me to give you a healing?" He nodded.

I grounded his body, and without closing my eyes went into a clairvoyant space. I soon saw the energy that had triggered his asthma attack. It was dark, claw-shaped and grasped his third, fourth and fifth chakras. I used one of my psychic techniques called erasing to move the energy out. "OK, Jonathan, you can climb back in your space now."

I clairvoyantly watched him reown his space. His eyes got bright and with a slight smile he said: "Thanks mom, I love you." I tucked the covers around him, gave him a kiss and left.

An hour later I got another phone call from him. This time his breathing was clear and his amusement back. He said, "Mom, I wish you hadn't done such a good job healing me. I didn't want to go to school tomorrow."

Rev. Lourdes Gonzaga

ANOTHER DAY IN THE LIFE OF A PSYCHIC

 "Michael," Susan Bostwick called, "I think we ought to have a Bishop's Dinner. What do you think?"

I looked up from my paperwork, grinning. "Sure! Are you buying?"

"Well," she said, and she couldn't help grinning either. "I suppose so, if I get to choose the restaurant! So let's go to that Italian restaurant we missed last time."

So we drove off and I had settled back in my seat, thinking of noodles and other fine things, when Susan did a 180 degree turn and headed back in the direction from which we had just come. She pulled up in front of a little nondescript restaurant, shut off the engine and turned to me.

"Michael, you don't really care what type of food we eat, do you?" She didn't wait for my answer. "I've passed this little place a dozen times and I have a feeling that tonight's the night to try it; what do you say?"

Well, what could I say, when she was already opening the door? "As long as they serve noodles . . ."

Well, they did serve noodles, and we had a delicious meal and some great conversation. As I was beginning to consider a dessert, Susan became alarmed and pulled at my sleeve.

"Michael! You know CPR, don't you?"

"Um-hum."

"Well she needs you. Let's go." And before I could ask "Who needs me?" I was out of my chair and following her.

A woman was lying on the floor. One of her dinner companions was crying, "Kate, oh please Kate, be OK!"

Susan knelt by Kate's feet, put her hands on her ankles and started grounding her. The companion, Sara, looked at me and said, "I know she's had a heart attack, I just know it! Will you help her, please?"

So I called on my nurse's training and checked Kate out—she was not breathing and had no pulse. I propped her head up to clear her airway and began giving her cardiopulmonary resuscitation. After a short while, I knew I had to get her heart going so I thumped her on the chest. She took a couple of breaths, slowly opened her dazed eyes and asked: "What happened?"

"You passed out. I revived you."

"He did more than that, Kate! I just know you had a heart attack and this lady and gentleman saved your life. Oh, God Katie. . . ."

"Who are you?" Kate asked. She was finally coming back into her body and becoming more conscious.

"I'm Rev. Michael Tamura and this is Rev. Susan Bostwick. We're both psychic ministers and healers. I think you'll be OK now."

Meanwhile, Kate's husband, Harv, had been furiously giving orders into the telephone for an ambulance. Restaurant waiters had tried to act as if everything was taken care of and served food as usual. The management however, was frantic.

As we stood to leave, Susan handed Kate her business card and said: "Here's my card. If you have any questions about what we did or what we saw clairvoyantly, please call."

"Wait, please tell me now!" Kate exclaimed.

"Yes now, before Harv gets back!" said Sara, looking significantly at Kate.

"Well," Susan said, "have you been to the gynecologist recently?"

"Yes, just this afternoon," Kate replied.

"I noticed a lot of your doctor's invalidation in your space, so I removed it. What I saw as the energy cause of your passing out was that a baby being (that's a spirit who wants to be born) crashed into your space. It came in so strongly that it knocked you out."

Seeing that both Kate and Sara wanted to hear more, she continued. "I also noticed that while you were out of your body, you saw it as a great opportunity to try and reach a decision. You were trying to decide whether or not to leave your husband."

"I knew it," Sara exclaimed. "I knew you were thinking about leaving Harv! It's been bothering you for some time. You could have talked to me about it, Kate—I'm your best friend."

"Yes, it's true," Kate whispered in awe. "It's all true."

I had been using my clairvoyant abilities and nurse's training throughout this episode and could now see that Kate would be fine; all she needed was rest and time to assimilate the information we had given her. Apparently she had come to the same conclusion; she smiled at Susan and me and said, "Thank you so very much. I'm deeply indebted to you both. I think now that I'd like to go home."

I helped her to her feet and Sara supported her. Susan lightly touched Kate's hand, giving her some additional grounding, and said, "Feel free to use the card if you have questions later."

Kate and Sara departed and we returned to our table. We knew that the healing was complete, for as soon as Harv returned they had an argument. She declared that she was fine and he said that she couldn't be. He wanted her to get in the waiting ambulance.

We left them to resolve their problem and I was ready for a dessert now; maybe some ice cream. . . .

"Excuse us."

We looked up from our menu to see two women standing at our table.

"I'm Eugenie and this is Emily," said one of them. "We're both registered nurses and just wanted to come over here and congratulate you on your quick thinking and the excellent care you gave to that woman. We wanted to help her too, but we just couldn't move."

"Thank you. It was nothing," I replied. "Just another day in the life of a psychic!"

Rt. Rev. Michael J Tamura

TALKING TO SPIRIT

What happens when you answer the ringing in the ears with a "Hello, who are you and what do you want?" Talking to spirit can be a healing for both ends of the line. Spirit likes communication. When you have a conversation with spirit, somebody gets a healing.

THANK YOU, LEWIS

how does a being without a body express anger or a thank-you to a being who has a body? In November of 1984 the Very Right Reverend Dr. Lewis Bostwick experienced a rather dramatic and startling show of gratitude.

Here's what happened.

It was a usual Monday evening session of the Aesclepion Healing Program's trance medium training in San Rafael. The main room was packed with visitors, six of whom had scheduled appointments for healings from the trance mediums. Lewis works in many ways with the trance mediums he's training. On this occasion, he sat "in line" and asked Rev. Michael Spencer to sit in front of him for a healing. He started to work on Michael. I was standing as a control behind Lewis and a little to the right.

After a few moments the energy shifted. Lewis suddenly moved his right hand up towards his neck. His gold neck chain popped off and fell across his open hand, placing the Egyptian cartouche pendant neatly on his palm. At almost the same time a gust of energy shot past me and through the wall behind me.

Lewis turned around beaming with excitement and asked me to refasten the chain. It was not until I started fastening the clasp that I became alarmed—it had a strong safety catch!

By way of explanation he said, "I saw it coming over here on its way out!"

Later, as no one else seemed to have seen what had happened, he further explained that he'd released a being that had been caught in Michael's space for many years. The being was very angry at having been stuck there. It was so glad to be free that it expended a surge of energy unfastening the chain and moving it into Lewis' hand as a way to say thank you. It then took off at great speed.

The chain holds a gold cartouche from the Church of Divine Man's 1984 religious pilgrimage to Egypt.

Its hieroglyphs read: "LEWIS—HEALER."

Rev. Marjory Horton

YOU BET!

Being a nurse in the Coronary Care Unit, I have witnessed and assisted at many a patient's health crisis and often death, usually by initiating CPR, giving medications and assisting doctors in placing the many tubes which monitor heart/fluid hemodynamics. And being a psychic, I also talk with the patient's spirit and let him know what is going on, showing him the alternatives. Usually I connect him up with the Supreme Being or another being who can help him through the crisis. One may think a nurse helps people live, but I find I also help people die, as people are more afraid of death than of life.

My favorite miracle-of-death patient was Bob. He came into our unit in a coronary crisis. His heart was so enlarged and damaged that it was not being an effective pump at all. Although he was sixty, he was very youthful and he did not want to die yet. I could see why. He was a professional gambler who loved going to the races and to Reno. He had great zest for life and loved to talk for entertainment. I thoroughly enjoyed taking care of him, seeing him slowly get better and finally walk out of the hospital.

Twice more he came back to us in a similar severe crisis. And each time he walked out a well man. The third time he came back, I thought, "OK Bob, this is it; now what are you doing?" I had quite a conversation with him on a spiritual level as we were pounding on his chest and placing the monitoring lines. I asked him if he wanted to die here and now and stop this game. He replied that he didn't, because he had so much more to do, but that his body wasn't able to keep up. I explained to him that he could let go of this body and get another one—but that he couldn't let go of his body easily here because the doctors would do everything in their power to prevent him. If he wanted to die, he could do it more easily and with more dignity where there were no doctors around.

He was a changed man after this conversation. His heart started beating on its own, and after twenty-four hours he was conscious and betting on his favorite pony in the Kentucky Derby. After a short hospital stay of two weeks, we wheeled him out to the car and to his daughter's care. As he was leaving, I called out to him, "Remember, Bob, I don't want to see you here again unless you are walking." He winked. "You bet," he said.

Time went on and we didn't see Bob again, but I knew he wasn't dead because I am a habitual obituary reader. It may sound morbid, but I find it interesting to note who has died. Finally, about four months after his last admission to the hospital, I saw his obituary. At work, one of the resident doctors related the story to me. At the time, the county fair was underway, and at the fair the local quarter horses and appaloosas run for the roses. Bob was at the track and had bet on his favorite pony. He was at the betting cages when the pony came in and he was handing in his tickets when he collapsed. This same resident doctor was the physician on duty at the fair that day and was called to come immediately. But when he got there, Bob had died and there was nothing the doctor could do to save him, so he had pronounced him dead.

Way to go, Bob! It was such a validation for me too, knowing that he and I actually did communicate on a spirit level and that he had heard me! He chose his death at the place he loved the best, doing what he enjoyed the most.

Rev. Patricia Borden

MATCHING ENERGY

Ο ne night I read a woman at the Berkeley Psychic Institute with whom I had so many similar life experiences it was almost like looking in a mirror. The first thing I saw was that she was an actress, which she validated with amazement. I also saw that she was extremely unhappy and had a lot of heavy energy in her space that wasn't hers. It looked like Russian energy. It was on a level of extreme poverty, oppression, low havingness, pain and punishment—the oppressed Russian peasant of about two hundred years ago.

As I was trying to describe this for her, I said it reminded me of a rather obscure Russian play about some incredibly miserable people who lived in a rat-infested, filthy, freezing basement. Amusingly enough, the play was called Tower Depths.

Well, when I mentioned the name of the play, this young woman was totally astounded because she had just finished acting in a production of that very same play! Being a very capable psychic, she had totally matched the energy level and low havingness level of her character in the play. And she hadn't known how to make separations so she was still carrying all that grief, pain and punishment around with her, wondering why she could hardly get out of bed in the morning.

When I pointed all this out to her from amusement, she changed her whole space. She became one thousand times lighter and brighter, and even found her own amusement level. She made a big step up in her havingness—and soon after that, she joined the Clairvoyant Training Program of the BPI.

Rev. Erica Leder

A MIRACLE WAITING TO HAPPEN

As a minister in a psychic church, I often experience clear telepathic communication with other ministers and students in the Seminary. But it still surprises me when I receive the same quality of communication from someone who hasn't been trained as a psychic, especially when that person is fully aware of the exchange. This was the case on a return flight from Canada last October.

I was sitting between two very attractive men. (Many years ago I had playfully created a mock-up to sit next to attractive men on airplanes to keep me out of boredom. My mock-up never fails!) I noticed immediately that I didn't like the man on my left, but my curiosity was piqued by the man on my right. I read a magazine for a little while until my eyes became tired. I closed my eyes to rest them. (When a psychic closes her eyes, watch out!) My attention turned to the gentleman on my right and I began to look at him as spirit; I looked at the energy around him and what he'd been up to lately. Within a few minutes, he put down his book and said, "Hello." (Later he told me that he had felt as if I had been talking to him without words and that he was compelled to find out who I was and how come he felt so naked in front of me.)

Then we began a conversation with words, covering practically every topic under the sun. After a couple of hours, I asked him unsuspectingly, "What do you do?"

He replied, "I design wheelchairs and skis for handicapped people."

"Oh, that's interesting," I said. "And a very odd profession. How did you get into that?"

"By being in a wheelchair myself."

I'm a little slow sometimes, and I still hadn't grasped what he was telling me. "How long were you in a wheelchair?"

"Ten years ago today." That time I heard. Wow! I had been talking to this man for two hours and hadn't noticed that he was crippled! He looked very healthy and, well, so . . . attractive. I was stumped. Come to think of it, I had noticed that I was communicating with him from the waist up, but hadn't paid much attention to it.

We talked some more. I found out that he had broken his back in a mountain-climbing accident in Colorado at age nineteen. I asked him a million questions: what did it feel like, was he happy, was he angry, why had he created that experience for himself this lifetime?

After some time, I began to feel sick, so I excused myself from the conversation, telling him I needed to rest. I went into trance and looked at my aura. He was plugged into me from all directions. Telepathically I asked him what he wanted from me. "A healing," came the reply.

Fair enough, I thought. I can do that. But first you'll have to pull your energy back so I have some room to heal you. He did.

I connected his body to the planet and said hello to him as a spirit. Immediately I saw a large tear in the back of his aura. After healing that, I moved on to the back of his solar plexus. There I saw a mass of tangled nerves, with little broken pieces in all directions, like a "SPLAT!" Below his solar plexus there was nothing; no continuation of nerve impulses. I began untangling this mess, snipping off the broken pieces and reconnecting the energy flow all the way down his spine. I grounded his sciatic nerves and cleaned them all the way down to his heels. I mended his feet chakras and ran earth energy through his legs.

Just as I was pulling back to survey my work and see if anything else needed to be done, he interrupted me. "What are you doing to me?"

I opened my eyes and looked at him in astonishment. I hadn't told this man I was a psychic, and for all apparent purposes I had been "resting." Yet he knew.

"I gave you a healing," I replied.

"Yes, I know," he said. "I can feel it. For the first time in ten years I can feel my legs! I can feel all the way down to my toes!"

Then ensued a conversation about healing and spirit and free will that lasted the rest of the flight.

•　•　•　•　•

In the next month, I saw Peter a couple more times. I gave him one more healing, with the same results. It was very obvious to me that he could heal himself of his handicap if he so chose. I could see all the stages of healing mapped out before me; the entire healing process was as simple and clear as his first healing.

If he so chose. I saw that as spirit he was holding back, gathering information, but not ready to allow that healing to happen. When I silently asked why, I saw that he had created quite a reputation for himself as an extremely capable man in spite of his handicap. He had created a very successful company, designing products for the handicapped and acting as a consultant to wheelchair companies. He had designed and built a beautiful house especially for his handicap, and still skied, kayaked, and sailed. He enjoyed the admiration he received for overcoming his disability in simple things, such as the way he wheeled that chair around, going down steps and skillfully maneuvering it as if it were a part of his body. At nineteen he had believed the medical opinion that his condition was irreversible, and had set out to prove himself capable anyway. He had done this, and was now reluctant to give up the validation he had received as a handicapped person. He was also afraid to compete in the world of those who walked.

I told him all this and he said very quietly, "That's true."

Oh, what frustration for a healer! It was very difficult for me to curb the tides of energy coming through my hands, and not heal him. Perhaps for him, it was enough to receive that hello on the tenth anniversary of his accident, a hello to him as spirit and all that he was creating, and a reminder that he had free choice.

Rev. Paula Camacho

CHRISTMAS BLESSING

Christmas Eve, 1980 was absolutely wonderful. I was six months into the Clairvoyant Training Program at the Berkeley Psychic Institute and really beginning to own my space and have lots of amusement.

An older couple, Buzz and Connie, were visiting at my parents' home. Sometime during dinner, they commented on how great I was looking. So the conversation turned to the BPI. I began talking about the program and gave them a little information on psychic healing. "Oh, faith healing!" exclaimed Connie. "Buzz, you should get one of those!" Connie is a strong Catholic. I noticed the grief in Buzz when she said this. "It might do him some good!" she confided to me.

When I inquired into the situation, I learned that because of the death of a twin grandson around Christmastime some eight years before, each Christmas had been more and more difficult for him to enjoy. His oldest daughter, Linda, who was also a high school friend of mine, had given birth to twin sons. Several months after birth, Linda had gone into the infants' room to find one of her sons with blackish colored skin. She had rushed him to the hospital, but he had died in her arms on the way. The diagnosis had been "crib death."

As Connie talked about it, I began to see how much this family was not just connected to, but totally stuck on that incident. Linda had been trying ever since to get pregnant again, but with no success.

"Let's drop the subject, shall we?" said Buzz, tears welling in his eyes. He quietly left the room.

I went to work.

Having known the family since childhood, I have tremendous affinity for them. I decided to do a silent healing while Buzz was in the living room chatting with my own children. I ran some gold energy through my body and connected it to the planet. I began looking at Buzz's aura and saw that it had a huge layer of black energy with brown underneath it.

I called in my healing masters who then connected him both to the planet and to the Supreme Being. I saw that what he had been doing was trying to heal his daughter with his grief energy. So I looked at Linda's baby-making machinery and at her female creative energy. Sure enough, her father's energy was all over it. No wonder she had not been able to get pregnant! I severed the cords of energy between them, brought their spiritual contract into present time, cleared out their spaces and brought in their highest levels of affinity.

In Linda's space, there was a lot of guilt energy. She was totally stuck on the picture that she had created the child's death. When I looked at the dead child, I saw that the being who had been in that body had not wanted to share the mother's affinity with the twin and so had decided to drop its body. I gave that being a healing too.

• • • • •

Very amusingly, three months later in a dream, Linda informed me that she was pregnant. Two days after that, my mother said to me, "Guess who's pregnant? Linda!" We both laughed; and noticing my secret grin, Mom said, "I should have known you would already know!" So I told her about my dream.

• • • • •

Recently I attended "Baby Colleen's" shower and had to laugh at the picture that mother Linda was putting out. It was "the trip to Ireland" that had gotten her pregnant after all those years!

I felt very validated; especially a month later, when I saw Linda, son Sean and daughter Colleen; and Colleen gave me a big "hello" and a "thank you." I laughed because the same being had made a return trip to this family. Only this time, it had chosen a female body. Pretty clever, I'd say.

Rev. Ginger King

A PLAYGROUND FOR BEINGS

"**W**hen the man we were going to read sat down, I thought, "This guy is really gone. He's high on drugs." His head kept drooping and his eyes would half close and roll back in his head. I expected him to pass out, and sat there hoping that the Berkeley Psychic Institute's house control would come and end the reading, because the level of energy was so intense. But until that happened, I would bide my time, creating and destroying pictures of roses.

I was the only person sitting side chair in this reading, so Robert, the center chair, asked me to read the rose and the chakras. When I looked at this readee's rose, it was black. "When I look at your energy as a rose," I said, "I see a black rose. There are lots of spirits without bodies getting in your space."

"Yes, I know," he whispered.

When I looked for past-life rings around the stem of his rose, instead of simple rings of color, I was surprised to see large doughnuts—heavy, thick rings radiating energy. "When you look at your past lives," I said, "you totally go into them. The purplish black ring at the bottom of your stem is from your lifetime in Atlantis, when you were a sorcerer. You experimented on creatures and put spirits without bodies into your creations. Some of those spirits are now using you as a playground."

I felt the energy in the room change—some of the spirits were dancing around the room, particularly on the readee's head. I opened my eyes and saw his head wobbling, his eyes half-shut and unfocused; his skin was strangely discolored, as if he had a skin disease.

"Hello," I said. And he got back into his body.

Soon the Assistant Director of the Institute, Rev. David Pearce, came in with the house control and asked us to take a look at this man's past-life aura. It was flapping like a cape in the breeze. I saw that this man had wanted to have the kind of power that he'd had in Atlantis, so he'd gone back to look at that information and had become stuck in that past life, except that the beings he had played with were now playing with him.

"Can I ask a question?" gasped the readee. "If these beings are using me as a playground, why do they want me to kill myself?"

So David had us look at some of the beings we saw in this man's space. He was a composer of modern-day music on the piano; there was a group of composers who channelled through him at various times. The majority of the 200 or so other beings were on a very low vibrational level. One of them in particular seemed to be a demon—really big and crouching. I hooked it up to the Supreme Being and grounded it; I could hear it growl. There were some big snake-like beings too.

Once the first fifteen or so beings were moved out, this man's aura totally changed and he suddenly calmed down. His eyes cleared, the color came back to his face, and he regained control of his body movements.

"You have totally changed my life," he said at the end of the reading. I realized that we had—and I saw that he had planned to kill himself that day. But somehow he had got his body to the Institute for a reading as a last-ditch effort.

Rev. Beth Dunlavy

HAVING THE MAGIC

Receiving a hello from a child has always been a wonderful thing to me. Recently, however, I've really seen how much my saying "hello" to the spirit of a child can be a miracle.

One day when I was tutoring in the home of one of my Yin Yang Seminary students, a miracle occurred. I was doing a meditation with a one-year-old. We created a bubble around the child, giving his energy back to him with tickles and magic sparkles. As we did this, the child sat in my lap smiling from ear to ear, loving every minute of it. We then reached up with our hands bringing in a gold sun. I told him to fill himself in with his own gold energy, some magic sparkles and a secret wish just for him.

As we did this, his father's energy came into the room, saying, "No. You can't have any magic!" The child stopped. On a telepathic level, I showed him the picture of "You can't have any magic." At once, he destroyed it. Then he grinned and continued filling himself up with gold and magic sparkles.

He sat there on my lap in his brilliant gold bubble, then, smiling, he leaned over, put his head on my shoulder, and on a being level said, "Thank you." To him, it was a miracle. He had received my "hello," destroyed the non-permission picture from his father, and he knew he could have magic.

Telepathically, he asked me for a kiss. I hugged him and kissed him on the forehead. We both smiled and for a minute we were in total spiritual communication.

Rev. Rosanna Taylor

FISHING IN HEAVEN

One summer I was at my cousin's house in Ogallala, Nebraska, and I asked her if she had any questions that I could look at clairvoyantly. We were good friends and it took her no time at all to think of a question.

Her best friend's twelve-year-old son, Bruce, had died the previous year. "How is he doing as a spirit?" she asked.

What I saw was very interesting. He was stuck as a spirit. I looked at what his mock-up had been for his life and saw that he had wanted to look at the dichotomy of perfect body/deteriorated body. He had been a straight-A student, very athletic, and liked by everyone. He had died of leukemia. The way this had come about was that as a child, he had protected his mother from his grandmother's energy. He had become stuck in that energy—the anger, jealousy, hatred and competition. It had destroyed his body, and even now as a spirit he still had his grandmother's energy in his space.

On a spirit-to-spirit level, I let him know that he could move that energy out. He heard me; immediately he became enraged, kicked her energy out of his space, and was free.

My cousin said, "How is he doing now?"

"Well," I answered, "if there is such a thing as fishing in heaven, that's what he's doing!"

"But that was always his very favorite thing to do!" said my cousin in amazement.

We laughed because Bruce had gained his spiritual freedom and could now take his next step.

Rev. Carol McCarthy

HAVE I GOT A MIRACLE FOR YOU!

When I was in the Clairvoyant Training Program and learning to validate my healing abilities, my eighty-five-year-old grandmother was admitted to the hospital—again. Now Bea wasn't just your average frail old lady. She was the typical—stereotypical—Jewish grandmother. Guilt, suffering, control, sitting in the dark—the whole bit. Needless to say, she had been "dying" for about twenty years and it was getting difficult for me to take all her moanings and groanings seriously. This time, however, was different.

After a week, the doctor took her out of Intensive Care, removed the respirator, and stopped making adjustments to her pacemaker. "She's not responding to the heart medications," he said, "I'm afraid I can't offer much hope."

I knew I needed to see my grandmother, and as I drove to the hospital, I decided to use my abilities of clairvoyance and psychic healing. I began by communicating with her. "Noni, if you want me to come and see you, you need to help me find a parking place." On my second run around the block, a car pulled out right in front of me. This wasn't too surprising. My grandmother had always been good at getting what she wanted.

As I entered her hospital room, I was greeted by the angriest-looking spirit I had ever seen. My grandmother was vibrating at a dull red color, about four feet above her body. I found my amusement (another psychic ability) and said "hello." I took her hand and grounded her body. Noni was very weak and her throat was raw from the respirator, but she very clearly said, "I can't live and I can't die." I asked her if she wanted a healing and she said, "No, I don't want to get better." I explained that the type of healing I had in mind involved clearing out the energy which kept her from seeing her next step. Much to my surprise, she agreed.

I sat down and went into a light trance. First, I grounded myself (extra, heavy-duty, industrial strength, amused, no-effort grounding); then I grounded the room, and while I was at it, I grounded the whole hospital. I called in my healing master and asked him to help me keep my grandmother grounded and to help me create a safe space in which to do the healing.

Next I established a spirit-to-spirit communication with my grandmother by sending hellos to her as a spirit. Clairvoyantly, I saw lots of fear and family energy between my grandmother and her body. She couldn't even see her body, let alone her next step, there were so many considerations from other people in her way. I grounded away the family's energy, attention and prayers that were imprisoning her. As a spirit, my grandmother became brighter and I helped her to communicate with the God of her Heart, the Supreme Being and her Akashic Record Keeper (not necessarily in that order). As she received this communication as an eternal being, she began to release some very Jewish programming which denies the existence of spirit. This was quite a step for a woman who had believed all her life that she was just a body.

I completed the healing by filling her space up with her own energy and information, and by making separations from her. As I stood to leave, she was sleeping. I kissed her goodbye, and assured her that whatever path she chose was okay with me.

The next morning I received a call from the hospital. My grandmother had taken her next step.

Rev. Cindy Dunn

"BE A MINISTER!"

1 t was Thanksgiving. I had no family in the Bay Area, so Mary, a woman I work with, decided to adopt a psychic for the day. I was about to go out the door, but first I said hello to Mary as spirit, and saw that she was wanting something from me. So I telephoned, thinking she needed half-and-half or something.

She said, "Cindy, my favorite uncle has had a stroke and he's in a coma. Can you give him a healing?" I said, "Sure."

I sat down at home and started to do a long-distance healing. Immediately I saw that he was in great pain. So I asked the Supreme Being to come in and communicate to both of us. The Supreme Being came in and said hello to the uncle; the uncle then died! I sat there in psychic shock. "What happened?" I asked guiltily. The Supreme Being said the relatives had been keeping him from taking his next step, but when that hello had reached him, he had been able to do what he wanted to do.

"What do I do next?" I asked. The Supreme Being said, "Be a minister." So I said hello to the uncle's spirit and gave his body a healing. I gathered his energy from this lifetime and gave it back to him. The hello I received from the uncle was enthusiastic! He was ready to move on and gladly accepted this communication from me and from the Supreme Being.

When I arrived at Mary's place, she greeted me with, "Cindy, my uncle died!"

"I know," I said. What validation! So, for Thanksgiving I got to give thanks for being a psychic and a minister in the Church of Divine Man.

Rev. Cindy Stakes

HELLO, KIDS!

1 was teaching fifth period physical education to thirty fourteen- and fifteen-year-old boys and girls. Most had their energy revved up, ready for action, while others were in total apathy, wishing they were at home in front of the TV. In fact, most of them were elsewhere, although their bodies were there. Trying to communicate with them, let alone get them to learn some badminton skills, was like talking to a dragon with his tail on fire, or to a Sleeping Beauty.

After a few days of total chaos, I was in desperate need of a new approach. So each day as I took roll, I would say hello to each of them, one at a time. Needless to say, they thought I was a bit peculiar, and started jeering at me and at each other. They couldn't quite figure out why in the world I was taking time to say hello—to do this silly thing.

After a few days of the same ritual, a noticeable change took place. They would wait for their turn and usually respond with a smile. They began to actually look forward to hearing their name and getting the hello, because it helped to bring them back into their bodies. Finally someone was acknowledging them as an individual. This was quite different from the "communication to the herd" approach which they were used to.

In the following days, I found them more enthusiastic about

being in class and more willing to listen and participate. They started saying hello to me before class and goodbye when leaving. A feeling of mutual respect began to grow.

I had this class for four weeks. What started out to be a battle turned into an enjoyable experience. Even now, several months later, they still say hello when I see them. Amazing what a hello to spirit can do!

Rev. Toni Clark Schlessinger

ONE HOT MIRACLE

1 was at the Berkeley Psychic Institute of Berkeley, sitting and running my energy when I had a premonition and then heard a very tiny noise in one of the back rooms. I looked up and saw the reflection of a man in the door. I moved quickly, but not quickly enough, and so I didn't catch up with him until he reached the end of the driveway. I yelled after him, "I hope you don't have anything that doesn't belong to you." He turned and said "No, man. Check me if you want to, man, go ahead." Although I kept seeing a picture of my wallet in my head, I didn't see any odd bulges when I looked at his body, and, being a small blond woman, the thought of frisking such a large black man didn't exactly appeal to me.

I went back inside and immediately checked my purse. My wallet was gone. This made me very angry. So I sat down, grounded my wallet, and filled it up with my gold energy and my ownership. I saw that the wallet was growing very hot in his hands, and he was moving it from hand to hand as if it were burning him. It made me laugh because I realized why stolen things are called "hot"—it's because of all the owner's anger. Now he was looking at the wallet very strangely, like "Oh-oh, what have I done?" So I grounded him and communicated to him as a spirit. I told him he could have the money but that he'd better give me back the wallet, identification, checks, and credit cards. I also saw in his aura that he had some fear pictures about voodoo. I let him know that I knew all about voodoo and how to use it.

When I told him to get my wallet back to me somehow, I thought perhaps he'd drop it in a bush, and that someone would find it and mail it to me. So imagine my surprise when five minutes later I heard a very timid knock on the front door. I opened it and there he was, towering over me.

As he handed me my wallet I noticed his hands were shaking. What a miracle! A thief bringing back what he had stolen! There really is no such thing as a victim!

Rev. Paula Camacho

REBIRTH

Having a breakthrough spiritual experience, something that turns your life around 180 or 360 degrees, can cause you to come into your body in a completely new way, seeing the world through a clearer, wider window.

"HE THAT HATH EARS, LET HIM HEAR!"

hearing a simple truth for the first time is always a miracle. My first Meditation Class at the Berkeley Psychic Institute was taught by the Rt. Rev. Karen Tamura.

One of the first things she said in class was, "You are not your body." This simple truth put me in one of the greatest growth periods of my life. For weeks, when I ran my energy in meditation, I would grapple with that statement and observe, "I am not Carol Tracy. I have had many names. Carol Tracy is the name given to this body that I as spirit am using in this life."

I tried to tell this truth to everyone I knew and thus learned my first lesson about people who can't hear. I lost many friends, and ended a marriage on the basis of this truth. What an incredible experience! It makes some of Jesus' statements very clear and some of the anger of non-believers in the Bible more understandable.

Pretty funny that one sentence can be so exciting to some and so threatening to others!

Rev. Carol Tracy Cullinen

REBORN

Two weeks ago, I received a healing from the Rt. Rev. Michael Tamura and nothing has felt the same since. He removed a guru from the center of my head.

This guru had jumped from my friend, who was his follower,

into my head and had proceeded to hide behind the drug energy I already had in there. His presence gave me a headache.

"That guru owns most of your brain!" said Michael in amazement. "How do you manage to think at all?"

"Think?" I said. "What's that?" It was very hard to laugh too, because whenever I had looked at the center of my head, all that was visible was the pain; therefore, avoiding it, I had quickly looked at something else! But Michael looked behind it and flushed this guru out, and as he worked he gave me a laughing commentary on where I was—in my body or out of it. Trying to come back into my head, I would run into that pain—and out I'd go again! Each time, I released more of the pain and unconsciousness and finally, I came into my head and stayed there.

What a miracle! Seeing, creating, destroying, having and feeling have all come back to me as I have re-owned my space. Problems? Nonsense! Nothing is insurmountable—I'm here in my body! I feel like a child, reborn. I have a body to play and laugh in. It is all so simple!

Rev. Janice Siebert

SCREAM OF FIRE!

F or as long as I can remember, I have had a scream of fire inside my head. I never understood it. As I remember, it began physically for me when I was four years old by creating extraordinary temper tantrums. I lashed out at anything around me, but mostly at myself. "It" was in there somewhere, but I could not find it. My parents did not know what to do with me so they took me to a doctor. "She has terrible tantrums," they told him. "She pulls her hair and bangs her head. She screams and destroys even her favorite toys!"

"It's just part of growing up," said the doctor. "She'll outgrow it."

Well, eventually I did stop my tantrums but only to create other destructive ways of coping with the intense frustration I felt. I had a strong image of wanting to turn my head inside out to somehow vent it. I wanted to find peace in my war.

I am very stubborn and have followed my intuition in moments no one else could comprehend. One of these intuitions was to drop out of college in North Carolina, get some money together and move to California.

When I heard about the Berkeley Psychic Institute, I immediately went there, and I knew that this was where I could find ME. One day when I arrived to take a beginning class, I found it was cancelled and the house control asked me to be a scribe in an aura reading. In the first half, I had a lot of fun drawing and coloring the aura. After the break, the reading control asked me if I would like to sit in line with the readers.

In the next five minutes, with the help of the control, I found the center of my head and everything fell into place for me. The scream of fire died down as I brought my own energy into this magic place, the driver's seat of my space. The frustration melted away. I cannot begin to describe the joy and release that enveloped my spirit. For the first time, I knew where I wanted to be! Here was the "it" that I had been looking for! I knew I had found my home, a place where I could learn and share and create my peace.

Anonymous

LIFTING THE CURSE

The miracle that I remember most vividly was in connection with a reading I had from the Rt. Rev. Michael Tamura, in which I found out that for most of my life I had been the effect of a curse. It was an especially powerful curse because I myself had created it in a previous lifetime.

I had been a Spanish Jew who did not wish to be converted to Catholicism by the Spanish Inquisition, and I had died swearing aloud that I would never, never be anything but a Jew. It had stuck, and accordingly, I had been a Jew for several more lifetimes!

As Michael described several of my past-life pictures, finally arriving at this curse, I had strong physical reactions. At first I felt spaced-out and nervous, and experienced cold-sweating palpitations, shortness of breath, and other minor signs of fear and impending death. Michael and his side-chair readers all joked and laughed, keeping good separations from my discomfort—my own amusement was nowhere in sight at that point!

Finally Michael decided to work on this curse and as he started to bring it all back into present time, the room grew quieter and quieter. Suddenly my body broke out into a profuse, hot sweat which continued for nearly forty-five minutes as Michael worked in silence. I couldn't talk, and when he was done and I got up to leave, I found I could hardly walk. I felt as if I had been compacted into my body. (I had been!)

• • • • •

Later that night, as I lay in my bed, I realized that I had accomplished the goal I had set and failed to reach in every lifetime since that Jewish one: to liberate myself from the curse. As I lay there, I asked myself, "OK, now what do I do?"

My heart stopped beating. I stayed very calm, realizing that I had a choice: to leave this body and eventually get another one; or to be "born again" into this body, which was one that had already amassed some experience.

After a few moments, I decided to continue in this body, and as if nothing had happened, my heart resumed its beating.

Ever since then, life has been simpler, easier and more fun. Even when there appears to be no reason to laugh, I am able to find my amusement. We really do create our own reality!

Rev. Jack Caldwell

BEING WITHOUT THE BEINGS

 s a child I was always terrified of the dark, even though I shared a room with my older sister. When I went to bed, I would lie on my back so I could see anything that might come at me. I would lie there in a cold sweat, not daring to fall asleep until my sister came to bed. When I tried to tell my parents I was afraid, they would assure me there was nothing to be afraid of and that nothing could hurt me. I knew they lied.

Even as an adult, I had an unreasonable fear of dark rooms and of being alone in the house at night. After I saw The Exorcist, it was all over between sleep and me. I even went to see a psychiatrist, but quickly realized that he knew nothing that I didn't know.

Eventually I became a student in the Berkeley Psychic Institute's Clairvoyant Training Program and my fear lessened, but there were still those nights when I knew I wasn't alone, even though mine was the only body in the room. I now know that it wasn't my imagination and I wasn't crazy. There were other beings around. Ugly ones. Nasty ones. In limitless numbers.

I looked forward to the first Spirit Guide lecture the way some people look forward to getting married or buying a house. The first night I learned to exorcise beings, I started by clearing out my house and I haven't stopped since! Nor have I been afraid of the dark! There is no longer anything for me to be afraid of because I can own my space, use my tools, communicate with the Supreme Being and get rid of those ugly nasties.

That lecture changed my entire life. That's what I call a miracle!

Rev. Jane Eagle

TURNING OFF THE TV

Unless I was very exhausted or very drunk, I used to see cartoons whenever I closed my eyes. I didn't like seeing cartoons. For one thing, they were in black and white; and for another thing, they always featured cats chasing mice or some such silly thing. I put off sleeping and drank a lot. I didn't want to close my eyes and see cartoons.

My second class at BPI was Beginning Meditation. In one of the first sessions, we were asked to create an image of a rose in front of us and explode it. I saw that rose, and I saw it go away when I exploded it. The teacher asked us to put different images into *roses and then explode them. So I put the cartoons in a rose and blew them up.*

Suddenly, I saw a picture of myself as a baby, staring at a television. The television and I were very still while all around there was a lot of movement and turmoil. I put this picture in a rose too and blew it up. Then I found myself feeling both lighter and more solid, and I was pleased with my control.

Since then, I haven't seen any cartoons. I also find I can remember much more of my childhood, whereas previously I could remember only a few scenes before junior high school. I even take naps sometimes! And now I draw cartoons for my own amusement, something I'd never done before.

Rev. Dennis McCarthy

FROM SOLON TO HEALER

I n 1973, I was elected to the San Jose City Council. I was planning to run for Mayor in 1978 and in that five-year time period, I worked towards it and amassed over $150,000 in the bank. As the election approached, my stomach hurt more and more, so that I wondered if I was developing an ulcer. After a little while, I noticed that I was afraid of winning the election! I sat down and did some thinking and had to admit to myself that I was disenchanted with the process of city government—tired of the game-playing which avoided solving any of the city's problems. The week before the election, I called a press conference and announced that I was withdrawing my candidacy.

What to do now? I drove down into the Santa Cruz mountains and enrolled in a one-month massage class. One client after another said to me, "You know, there are many good massages being given around here, but when you touch me, it's a very different experience—my body changes."

"Hmm," I thought. "I wonder if I . . . ?"

One of the women there had taken a class at the Berkeley Psychic Institute of Santa Cruz. "They teach psychic healing," she informed me. "I think you might be interested."

"Hmm," I thought. "Could it be that I . . . ?" I drove down there and got an aura reading. Never in my life had I felt so good as I did after that reading! And how could these people know all those things about me? (I later found out that it had been done by beginning Clairvoyant Class students, not even advanced ones!)

I returned to the mountains for the rest of my massage training. The final test required each of us to give a massage to one of the teachers. The teacher to whom I was assigned told me before I started that her neck and shoulders were out of alignment, and had been for a long time, and that she lacked full range of motion in her head.

As I began the massage, I found that I couldn't take my hands off her neck and shoulder area. "I see red around your neck, and it looks twenty-one years old." Who said that? I stood with my hands on her neck, astonished at the unusual vernacular coming out of my mouth. For the first time, I was hearing myself speak. I was giving my first aura reading, without even knowing that's what it was.

"Oh," she replied, as if my reading her was normal. She easily identified the burden on her shoulders: "I thought I had gotten rid of him!" As my hands continued working on her neck muscles, she began having spasms. Soon she was crying, then screaming.

My hands stayed on her neck until finally she quieted. "Sit up, now," I said. I looked at her shoulders and they were straight. She turned her head and the full range of motion was there.

"But I can't let go of him as easily as that!" she said, and tightened her body up again. She was back where she had started.

"Lie down again," I said. I began working on her neck once more and we ·went through the same process a second time. After she quieted, I sat her up and saw that her neck and shoulders were aligned again. This time she let go and allowed herself to remain aligned.

"Hmm," I thought. "Maybe I have some healing ability!"

In the middle of my Beginning Meditation Class a few weeks later, I received a job offer. It was an appointment under the Carter administration in Washington, to be Director of Governmental Affairs with the Department of Energy. Yes, I took it. I was there for a year, until I lost the position when Carter was voted out.

So in 1981, I was back in Beginning Meditation, and then into the Clairvoyant Training Class. Now they can't get rid of me!

Rev. Jim Self

CREATING
YOUR OWN REALITY

When you are the master of your own universe, you create and destroy what you want: more havingness for money, spiritual growth, happiness, communication and even miracles.

A MOVING EXPERIENCE

Two of my mock-ups happened recently when my husband and I were moving from an apartment to our new house. First I had mocked up a two-bedroom house in a safe, quiet neighborhood, with the following: a fireplace, storage area, garage, laundry, hardwood floors, great neighborhood, and rent under five hundred dollars. We got all of those things at an unbelievable rent of four hundred twenty-five dollars!

Then, when it was time to move, I felt we needed another man with a lot of motivation to help lessen the burden on everyone else. So I mocked up someone with enthusiasm to come over and help; I specifically mocked up someone who WANTED to help! Within half an hour, I was delighted when a friend who was helping us move reported that a man walking by had stopped to ask if he could help us!

This man, whom we had never seen before, made endless trips up and down forty stairs carrying heavy boxes, and he did it with boundless enthusiasm and energy! He worked until our truck was full. I thanked him and tipped him; he went happily on his way and we relaxed in our great new house!

Rev. Nancy McWethy

A MOCK-UP IN FOUR FIGURES

Cash flow was tight. I was tired of being broke, so I sat down and mocked up a check. One thousand dollars would be nice. A round number. I meditated, flowing earth and cosmic energies through my channels, and polishing up my creative space. Setting up the mock-up was fun. I envisioned a check made out to me, my name spelled correctly, March 1985 as the date (it was then late February), the amount, and a valid signature. I stipulated that it had to be a real check, something I could take to the bank and cash; not one of those Publishers Clearinghouse promotionals. And I didn't care where it came from, except I didn't want any relative to die and leave me something.

Then I forgot about the mock-up.

The next week I went to my Post Office box and there was a check for twelve hundred dollars! Made out to me! (My name was even spelled correctly.) It was from the United States Treasury, dated March 1st, 1985. With no explanation. I cashed it immediately (after xeroxing it), and then discovered it was an income tax refund from four years earlier that I had never received. Originally the refund had been a much smaller sum, but it had quietly accrued interest over the years.

Rev. Kate Keilman

MOCKING UP A MANSION

1 had reached a point of desperation with my living situation—sharing a house with a perfect stranger. True, he was perfect (a male) and God knows he couldn't have been stranger. So I resolved to move. I found a new place and gave notice, but then discovered that there was no way I could possibly bear to live in my intended new space. I wasn't moving forward, and I couldn't go back. It was from this backed-into-a-corner position that I created my house mock-up.

First I meditated and ran my energy for three hours straight.

This really cleaned out my space so my creative center started to vibrate. Toward the end of this cleanout I asked myself a few questions about my situation and got some great answers. Then I created my mock-up, just the way I wanted it—and really owned it. When I was finished I decided to do something good for my body—get a massage.

Psychics work in strange ways. I found myself in Piedmont instead of Berkeley having this massage. Upon finishing, and knowing that I've gotten lost every time I've been in Piedmont, I decided I'd tough it out and try to figure out once and for all how to get out of Piedmont.

The first thing that happened was that I ran into a mailman. I asked him my favorite question, the one I'd been asking all the mailmen in my own neighborhood. "Do you know of any places for rent?"

In my mind this seemed kind of funny. There I was in Piedmont, surrounded by these forty-room mansions. No way could I afford to rent one of these. I couldn't even afford to rent a two-bedroom place in my own part of town. No problem for a psychic though, so why not ask?

Well, as it turned out, the mailman's information led me to a person who told me that the whole top floor of her mansion would be available for rental in twenty days. She had no plans to advertise the vacancy, but was I interested?

My mock-up was for a three-bedroom house, about 2500 square feet, in a good section of town, with a great landlord, for $650 a month. What I got was a three-bedroom flat, 3500 square feet, in the best section of town. And although it was $25.00 more than I wanted to pay it also included laundry, utilities, a hot tub, large swimming pool, and occasionally a maid. What could I say? I decided I could deal with the extra twenty-five dollars. And of course, do you know what my first conversation with my new landlord was about?—psychic things. I guess she had had a mock-up for me too. Amazing what a good cleanout and a clear mock-up can do!

Rev. Dona Wessells

CREATING A WAY TO THE LECTURE

"That important lecture in January is really going to be difficult to get to," the voice inside my head informed me, "and there's no way of getting off early from work." In spite of this conviction, I sat down a few days before the weekend, opened up my space, created a mock-up, and then forgot about it.

That Friday evening of the first lecture, I was scheduled to work until 6:15 p.m.; this would make me late to the lecture as I was coming from San Francisco and it would take at least an hour to get to Santa Rosa. I had given up. At 5:25 I wasn't even thinking about leaving. I was resigned to my fate when one of the guys at work—a person I hardly ever spoke to—walked up to me and said, "Hey, if you want to leave early, go ahead. I'll cover for you." I left and nearly fell over on the way to my car as I remembered the mock-up I had created—and just received! Hurray! It's just that simple.

Rev. Kathryn Wilson

A MERCEDES MOCK-UP

My husband Terry and I were about five months into the Clairvoyant Training Program. We were doing a tremendous amount of commuting, and we thought we might enjoy a spiffy car.

My boss mentioned one day that they were going to sell one of the company's Mercedes and asked if I would like it. My answer was an immediate "Yes!" Now all we had to talk about was price. The talk began at $12,000, about $1,000 under the lowest blue book price.

I talked with Terry and we decided it was too much. Then my boss went down to $11,000 so we began negotiations with our credit union.

We decided to use our psychic tools, and we set an $8000 grounding cord on the car deal. The first thing that happened was that although we had asked for a lot more, our credit union would lend us only $7,500. Whoops! Other people can see grounding cords too! So we changed the pictures. We continued to show the company an $8,000 picture, and we set a $9,500 grounding cord on the credit union.

After a few days my boss called me into his office and asked me how I would like the car—for $8,000!

The next day the credit union agreed to lend us the money— and had increased the amount to $9,500!

Rev. Lorren Toner

SWIMMING WITH DOLPHINS

1 learned about mock-ups in my Beginning Meditation Class at the Berkeley Psychic Institute. The teacher told us to try a mock-up, if we wanted to. I'm sort of contrary in nature, and I wanted to see for myself if there was anything to all this psychic stuff I was learning. I decided to mock up something I didn't think I could possibly have, but which I really wanted.

I had always had a fantasy of swimming with a wild dolphin free in the ocean. I had read a lot about dolphins for years, and wanted to have some experience to match up with all the book information. It seemed like total fantasy—how could it ever come true? I created the mock-up, and then put it out of my mind because I considered it so remote from my existence.

Within a week a friend mentioned that a person she knew had made arrangements to be at sea with some people studying wild dolphins. She said these people were looking for participants. I made a few phone calls, and the people told me they'd like me to come along on the trip planned in a couple of months.

This gave me enough time to learn to use scuba equipment, and make all the other preparations. A few months later, there I was, in a warm ocean surrounded by curious, lively dolphins. I was utterly astonished and fabulously pleased to have created this unlikely experience!

Rev. Edee Howland

ON THE ASTRAL

What happens when you leave the body? Out of body experiences can be tremendous adventures.

A DREAM MIRACLE

1 wanted, while dreaming, to have more awareness that I was in my astral body. Late one evening, I lay down in bed and began running my energy. It flowed easily through my body. As the minutes passed by, my awareness increased of myself, the spirit, resting easily in this body of millions of cells, safely, cozily held in physical time and space. I was connected to the core of the planet and to the cosmos. Soon I was floating above; from this vantage point, I could feel the physical sensations in my body—breathing, heartbeat, head resting on pillow—at the same time as being a free-floating spirit. The usual feeling of time passing by changed to one of being immediately present.

A thought appeared in my mind, of being on my folks' front lawn at their beach house on the northern Oregon coast. Instantly I was there! The grass tingled my feet. I knew the time to be two or three in the morning. The house and garden were easily visible, glowing slightly; I admired the new appearance of the house, the result of some remodeling I had done a few years previously.

Another thought appeared, of walking to the lawn's edge for a closer look at the beach below. Instantly I was there! As I gazed around, a red glow appeared on the horizon, faint at first, and gradually expanding to the sky above. I thought of waking my sleeping folks to see this colorful celestial event. Again, the thought was sufficient, and there they were walking towards me, gazing skyward, mouths and eyes wide. The sky was fully aglow now. Shimmering crimson curtains of light undulated in a cosmic breeze. Our skins shone red. The ocean sparkled. Awestruck, we broke into smiles of delight! Communication happened easily, just by thinking and knowing. God was smiling at us and laughing with us!

Slowly the glow softened and dimmed. Stars reappeared. A cool breeze quickened, encouraging Mom and Dad to return to bed. I remained, untouched by the wind. When the coming dawn began to fade the starlight, I decided to leave.

My eyes popped open! It was early morning and a powerful well-being filled me. Life that day was fun and effortless. That evening, I called my folks to tell them about my dream. As soon as the word, "Hello," left my mouth, Mother started in talking— very unusual for her. "We had the most incredible experience last night!" she exclaimed. "We woke up about 2:30 a.m., wide awake, knowing we had to go and look outside. We did. The sky was all red! It looked like the Northern Lights. Great, bright curtainy waves of red shimmering above, lighting up our faces! It really seemed as if you were there too! We kept feeling your presence, as if you were watching the show with us!"

I told them about my dream. Much excitement and exclaiming followed . . . Yes! It was real. As spirit, I was really there, in my astral body. We all shared total, validating enthusiasm. What a great healing!

Rev. William Prince

"THIS IS HOW YOU DO IT!"

a bout three and a half years ago, I sat in a cabin on the border between Sweden and Norway; I was four months pregnant and staring in frustration at the cotton thread and tiny crochet hook in my hand, trying to figure out how to make lace.

My Scandinavian friends had gone off to climb the mountain that day and dig garnets out of the rock cliffs; all but two men who were sitting at the kitchen table talking politics.

I had been drawn over and over to the beautiful hand-made lace that is traditional in Scandinavia, especially to the lace-trimmed baby sheets. Finally I had found a store that sold the thread and tiny hooks. On this special day, I was trying my best to copy a piece of lace or make up a pattern of my own. Finally I gave up and lay down to take a nap.

In my dream a little boy came to me from over a mountain and through a mist. He looked about three years old, had curly blond hair and blue eyes. He walked quickly and with confidence. He seemed happy to see me but a little impatient, as though he definitely had more important things to attend to. He took the needle and thread from my hand. "Hello," he said. "My name is Michael Olaf and this is how you do it." Very quickly he showed me the stitches, then handed the work back.

I woke with a start, got out of bed and rushed across the room to the lace materials, shouting, "I know how to do it!" to the astonished men still sitting at the kitchen table. By the time my friends returned from their mountain climb, I was well on the way to a lovely piece of lace. They couldn't believe it.

Later, back in Stockholm, I phoned Jim, my husband, in California, and told him that our child was indeed a boy and that he had told me his name. Jim approved. "Michael" is his own middle name; "Olaf" was the name of five kings of Norway and St. Olaf is the country's patron saint. Jim is Norwegian.

The piece of lace is now sewn onto a linen baby sheet for Michael Olaf who sometimes acts the part of reigning monarch.

Rev. Susan Macylin Stephenson

THE NECKLACE OF AMBER

1n November of 1981 I was doing a healing on a student before teaching Beginning Meditation Class that evening. She wore a large amber teardrop necklace, which I admired. I said how much I liked amber, and wasn't it a wonderful thing. Not too far away from us was Rev. Jim Tarzan, who was a student in the Clairvoyant Training Program. He was a championship chess player which was why we called him Boris. Well, pretty soon it was Christmastime and Boris came up to me and handed me a small, slightly shabby box. Wow! Was I surprised, *because inside was the most beautiful amber necklace I had ever seen, with a note saying he had gotten it while playing chess in Russia.*

• • • • •

A year later I went on holiday with my family. When we got to the hotel I took my necklace off and placed it in one of the bags. Two days later, when we were heading back, I felt as if something was missing. At our first pit stop, I quickly looked in the luggage for my necklace. Not there. When we got home I carefully took everything upstairs, and went through it all. NOTHING! Nothing in the car, and nothing at the hotel when I telephoned them. It was gone!

Every once in a while you have something that you can't quite let go of. That's how I felt about that necklace. A year went by and I would think about it occasionally, and be unhappy with myself. Not very bright losing such a great necklace! Grumble, mumble.

• • • • •

Almost a year later my second child, Nicholas, was born in October, 1983. It was a really easy, happy home birth, and when I fell asleep that night I had one of those very vivid dreams. I dreamed that I had gone away to find my amber necklace. When I found it, I stood there looking at it; I put my hands on either side of it and slowly it disappeared. Then I dreamed I was back in my bedroom; the necklace rematerialized, and I put it under my bed. I left it in a perfect circle directly beneath my head.

I woke up the next morning, and even with a new baby to take care of and play with, I couldn't get the dream off my mind. Still weak from giving birth the previous afternoon, I got up, rolled aside a hundred-pound, carved screen, and shoved aside a two-hundred-fifty-pound bed. Huffing and shaking, I looked beneath the bed where I had remembered the necklace being in my dream. I hoped no one would come in and ask me what I was up to, and I felt silly because I had cleaned or looked under the bed at least a dozen times during the past year. I looked and just stopped. There was the necklace. It was in a perfect circle. It was directly beneath where my head had been the night before. I sat down on the floor and picked up my necklace. I knew within myself that I had done this. I had given my necklace back to myself.

Rt. Rev. Karen Tamura

1

"I SEE WE HAVE MET BEFORE!"

had always silently laughed at those who wrote their dreams down and looked for some significance in them during their waking hours. Then I got a hello from Lewis on the astral.

One night, I went to sleep as usual. I dreamed that I woke up (something I had often done as a child) and that I walked along a road with a fence running next to it. As I moved along this road, I could feel the sun's heat and smell the dust. At the end of this road was a house with several people sitting on the porch. They were communicating and moving around independently of me, unconcerned with what I was doing.

I was greeted and invited in. I remember feeling a little nervous as I noticed that all of these people were smiling as though they knew something I didn't. I walked in and sat at a table around which maybe twelve other people were sitting. They smiled that smile. Even though no words were exchanged, there were very clear impressions being given. I was being invited to sit at the table with them, to play their game. It was one man in particular who was inviting me.

The meeting seemingly dissolved and I was returning down the road from where I had come, but with a person accompanying me on the other side of the fence. As we parted ways, I woke up, feeling happy and excited. I wrote for three hours—details of the people, insights I had gained about myself, feelings of relief and enthusiasm I had felt.

•　•　•　•　•

Two weeks later, I had an aura reading at the Berkeley Psychic Institute. I was excited about what I had been told and was waiting in what was called the Gold Room in the Institute for the Director to come and talk with me.

In walked the man who had invited me in my dream to sit at the table. He walked right out of my dream and into this room, or so it seemed. We talked about psychic abilities, the Institute, and what the Clairvoyant Program was designed to teach.

During this entire conversation, I couldn't tell whether I was dreaming or awake. I kept floating back and forth. I was so stunned by what I was experiencing that it never occurred to me to say anything about my dream or what was happening to me as I sat there.

The longer I sat there, the more numb and confused I became, until this man, the Director, paused and said, "Hello, I see we have met before!" He put his finger to my forehead, and I began laughing for no reason except that now I knew I was awake and I was enjoying talking with this person.

Yes, I received my first hello from Lewis Bostwick on the astral and had it validated two weeks later when I first met him in person.

I'm still laughing !

Rt. Rev. John Fulton

USING THE TOOLS

Honing and owning psychic tools such as grounding, running life force energy, finding the center of your head, creating and destroying mental image pictures can lead to a miracle—either for yourself or another—at work or at home. Once you own them, honing them is the key.

GROWTH PERIOD EXCELLERATION

I woke up one morning with a small jabbing pain at the base of my spine. Over the next four or five days it grew worse and worse. It felt like a pinched nerve and made it painful to walk. I also had a miserable cold. On Friday evening I was lying in bed, crying and making plans for a Saturday funeral.

Then I remembered a technique I had learned for accelerating a growth period. As I lay there in a stupor, I imagined running green energy throughout all of my energy channels. Both my earth energy and my cosmic energy were deep shades of green. It was all I could think about—green energy. After about twenty minutes I became aware of a swollen area at the base of my spine. A large blister had formed and, just at that moment, it broke open. All of the pus and blood drained out and the pain totally disappeared. I stood up and felt perfectly well; my congestion and headache were completely gone. I took a shower, got dressed, and even made it to my Clairvoyant Training Class on time!

Rev. Madeline Weise

TALKING TO THE SPIRIT OF THE LAW

One morning on my commute into San Francisco, I accepted a ride along with another commuter so that we could go through the car pool lane to the bridge. The lady driver was very anxious and obviously late and as we approached the Toll Plaza—even the carpool lane was at a stand-still. She became even more jumpy and decided to cut the traffic by driving on the hard shoulder, even though we had passed a Highway Patrolman just a few minutes before. Well, needless to say, in two seconds the Highway Patrolman was behind us and flagging us down.

I was rather late myself but I was also in some amusement about this situation. Our driver, on the other hand, was upset and angry and jumped out of the car to confront the policeman.

I decided to have some fun using my tools. So I started to say hello to my driver and the policeman as spirit. I grounded them both, hooked them up to the Supreme Being and gave them per-mission to have their own space. I watched as they started to find amusement about the situation rather than anger. A minute later, the lady jumped back into the car laughing and said, I don't know what happened! One minute we were shouting at each other and the next he said, 'I don't know why, but I'm not going to give you a ticket.' "

The other passenger said, "What a miracle!" I smiled to my-self. What a great way to say hello to myself as spirit at 8:00 a.m. on the way to work!

Rev. Sue Pearce

RING OF FIRE

1 n August of 1979, I was taking Beginning Medita-tion and Healing Classes at the Berkeley Psychic In-stitute of Santa Rosa. I was living on the coast, north of Jenner. Five miles inland, my Dad owned a forty-acre parcel on Gualala Ranch. In August, there was a heat wave and the woods were ex-tremely dry. Everyone was on edge, just waiting.

Sure enough, a forest fire broke out and I received a call from a friend whose place had burned. The fire was burning fast and had jumped the road. So I met up with a neighbor from Gualala Ranch, and with some others we headed for the Ranch to help. We had all been trained as volunteer firefighters.

As we drove, the fire on both sides of the road made it seem very small. We stopped at the first house on the Ranch, Janet's, which looked like Grand Central Station, with dozens of firetrucks, pumpers filling up at the reservoir, and fire blocks being built. We hosed Janet's roof and helped with pumping water.

Here we also met up with my brothers. No one had heard from my Dad; his property was at the end of the 2600-acre Ranch. So we drove on, trying to reach it. Everything in sight was burning and we didn't know what we'd find. We assumed that his house would be burning too. As we drove, we could see helicopters carrying huge buckets of water from a reservoir and dumping them.

Finally, on the road we found my Dad. He was helping his neighbor, Margaret. They had fifty-five-gallon drums of water, Indian backpacks, chain saws, boxes of sandwiches. His parcel was just beyond Margaret's place, and we could see that so far, it hadn't burned. Margaret's house was still being built and was almost complete. The Fire Department couldn't risk driving down her road—fire on both sides and they were busy setting a back fire. A group of us volunteered to go down with her to her house. We cut down trees, dragged them out of the way and hauled down a fifty-five-gallon drum of water. (All the water lines were made of black plastic pipes and had melted.)

We breathed the acrid smoke, listened to the crackling and popping, watched as whole trees burst into flames. It was as if some huge dragon were extracting his vengeance. We wore wet bandanas on our faces and Indian backpacks, going back and forth for more water. At one point we were very close to losing Margaret's house—steam rose from the wood as we poured water on the outside walls. At this point, no one knew whether the fire had jumped the road further down at my Dad's place—the road was only ten feet across.

I had always been afraid of fire—such a destroyer—yet I was experiencing total calm and inner strength. I prayed as I worked and I remembered Ecclesiastes—"a time for every purpose under heaven. . . ." We worked on past dusk.

• • • • •

In the morning, I rode with my Dad through the smoking, black landscape to check out his land. When we reached it, we stopped in total awe. It was as if a magic bubble had surrounded his parcel—everything was quiet and normal. We stood, enjoying the silence. I went into the garden; flowers grew, fresh and green. I picked a bunch and drove over to Janet's place with them. Her house was a pile of black rubble.

We worked for three more days; walking around, putting out sparks with shovels, wetting down hot spots. I knew I had experienced a miracle. Why hadn't my Dad's land burned?

• • • • •

Later, when I returned to a class at the Institute, I learned the answer. When the staff and students had heard about the fire, they had gathered together, gone into trance, and had done some healing work. They had grounded my Dad's property, surrounded it with a ring of protection roses, and placed a protective spirit, a Maria, above it. Twelve thousand acres had burned. Of the sixty-four parcels of land, my Dad's and the one next to it were the only ones saved.

Rev. Natasha Lynn

A LITTLE GOES A LONG WAY

A few Saturdays ago, I did a reading on a lady named Kat. As I looked clairvoyantly at Kat, I could tell she was a capable spirit. She was healing herself on emotional levels, and becoming more vigorous physically. However, the middle layer of her aura was dark grey and black. I saw that this was not her own energy, but that of a man a little older than she. I could see that this energy prevented her from liking herself, or from being able to give herself credit for her many abilities. It also had the effect of making her feel uncomfortable about expressing her own femininity. I asked if she had an older brother, or a relationship with someone like that. She said she didn't know whose energy I might be seeing. I let it drop.

About ten minutes later, Kat mentioned her ex-husband and

everything clicked together. The grey I had seen was his energy. Kat was amazed that his energy was still affecting her after so many years, but as I described its effect on her, she recognized what I was talking about. She accepted my offer to remove the energy from her aura, and without effort I cleared about eighty percent of it away. The healing took less than two minutes.

That was when the miracle began. With a little more freedom, and a little more space to like herself, Kat began to bring more and more of her own spiritual information into her awareness. I watched this process clairvoyantly. I saw her move a tremendous amount of her life-force energy from about two feet above her head right into her body. As she began to use this new energy, I saw every layer of her aura change color. Most of the colors became brighter, and more lively, which I saw as her gaining personal freedom and control of her own space. I had never seen quite so much change happen so quickly before.

Kat herself said she felt "rushes." Her facial expression and body posture began to relax. Soon she started to cry, and then to laugh. "It's been ten years!" she said. "I can't believe it!" We talked about what she was feeling, and I said that it looked as if she were remembering things she didn't know she had forgotten. "That's a good way to describe it," she agreed. Very rapidly, she moved a lot of ability from the abstract, spiritual plane into the concrete, physical plane; she "remembered" information she already had.

● ● ● ● ●

When I saw Kat about a month later, she looked wonderful. She had retained all the energy she had gotten back that Saturday and she was using it. She was clearly running much more female energy; she was well dressed and seemed more comfortable with herself. When she had walked in that Saturday, I would have described her as "apathetic." Now, a month later, she seemed to radiate enthusiasm and good cheer.

Witnessing this miracle taught me at least one good lesson as a healer. This had been one of the most profound healings I had ever seen, yet I did only the tiniest amount of healing (about two minutes' worth). The fact that this became a miracle had less to do with any miraculous healing powers that I might have than *with the fact that Kat was very ready to take some giant steps in her personal growth. All she needed was the little catalyst provided by some healing work on just one layer of her aura. I learned to give the people I counsel just the amount of healing that they can use to do what they want to do.*

Rev. Marc Shargel

VOODOO IN TAHITI

hen we were six months into the Clairvoyant Training Program, Janice and I went on a vacation to the Tahitian Islands.

Soon after we arrived at Bora Bora, a beautiful and very remote island, we met two of the employees of our resort: Paolo, the windsurfing instructor, from Uruguay, and Jacques, the Recreation Director, from France.

That evening, not thinking of what the consequences might be, we sat down in our hotel room to look clairvoyantly at the island and at these two men. I saw that Bora Bora was controlled by some old religious energy which was supposed to keep all the inhabitants safe, but which also attracted a lot of voodoo and "crazy" energy. When I looked at Paolo, I noticed a big cord of energy running into his space, which made my body feel uncomfortable. We talked about it for a while, gave each other a healing, and went out for some fun.

A couple of evenings later, we were talking to Jacques after dinner. "Where's Paolo?" I asked.

"Paolo!" said Jacques. "I do not know what happens with him. Each night now after dinner he is going to his room and nobody is seeing him. It is strange, yes?" While Jacques was talking, I looked clairvoyantly at Paolo's room and saw a black and silver funnel of energy running into the ceiling. But I thought no more of it, and went out for some more fun.

A couple of evenings later, Janice and I dined at the same table as the two men. That night there was a special menu and live entertainment afterwards. But as the musicians started testing their mikes, Paolo got up and left. Jacques rolled his eyes and moved over next to me. After the first song, when I turned round to Janice, her chair was empty. Didn't she like the show? I couldn't believe it—the musicians were so funny and having such a good time! But as the evening progressed, I grew first uneasy, then jittery, and finally in an outright panic, I bolted for our bungalow. What was wrong with me?

On her bed, I found Janice, very sick. She was vomiting, sweating and unconscious. Instinctively, I knew it wasn't a normal sickness and not knowing what to do, I went outside to walk around a bit and find my space. Sitting down on a rock, I grounded my body and said hello to myself repeatedly. As I began to feel calmer, I inspected my body; it looked OK. Good job! Using some more of my psychic tools, I sent a hello to Janice. She, the spirit, was on the bungalow roof. When I asked the question, "What's happening to Janice?" the Supreme Being showed me a line of energy running to Paolo's room and there I saw a voodoo doll and a lot of silver energy. I continued grounding out my fear and saying hello to myself, and when I felt a little more certain, I got up and returned to our bungalow.

Janice was sleeping quietly—but one glance at her brought all my fear flooding back! She didn't look like Janice! Her face was fat and contorted. Clairvoyantly, I saw that with Janice up on the roof, another being had entered her body. I saw a big cord to her crown chakra and black dots all over her body, especially on her face and solar plexus.

I hadn't done much healing work on the black dots before I realized that she had to do the rest. So I sat her body up and began to shake it. "Janice!" I called as I dragged her out of bed. "Janice! Own your space! Get up and run around!"

Slowly she came partly into her body. Her eyes focused and she got to her feet. As she screamed and ran, the energy around her body turned a fiery red. She yelled, "Get out of my body! Get out of my body!" Within a few minutes, the being was gone and Janice was back, saying hello to me.

As I did some more healing work on her, I saw that Paolo was aware of what he was doing and of his agreement with the being that came through him. It was an agreement that he had had for several lifetimes, but although he wasn't happy with it any more, he had no idea he could break it. I began communicating this to him as a spirit, but seeing what a lot of communication it would have taken to break up the game, and realizing it wasn't my problem, I ceased. Eventually we both got some sleep.

• • • • •

Next morning, the sky was blue and the green waves rolled peacefully to the sand as if nothing had happened. But we felt it was time to leave! When we boarded the boat for the next island, almost everyone on it was sick. I saw clairvoyantly that it had been the high level of energy work the previous night that had made them sick.

That day on our new island, I also became sick. My body was feverish and ached all over. I knew Paolo was playing with me now, but since I was aware of it, I was ready for him. Unable to move from my bed, I sweated through nine hours of high fever in a semi-conscious state, dimly aware at times of Janice beside me, but mostly dreaming intensely of past voodoo lives and struggling with fear. I became mean and tough as a spirit, claiming my space back, battling for my seniority. It was a long fight. When I woke in the evening, I lay for a few minutes enjoying my new well-being and feeling of strength. The tree frogs sang in the dusk and music wafted through our window from the direction of the beach. I looked over at Janice's dozing form in the chair. "Janice!" I yelled, jumping out of bed. "What are we waiting for! Aren't we here to have fun? Let's go out and dance!"

Rev. Laurna Gmelin

HOUSECLEANING

O ne night at the Berkeley Psychic Institute of Pleasanton, I gave a two-hour aura reading to a woman named Beth. At the end, instead of asking any questions, she told me about the apartment that she and her two daughters had recently moved into. "We all feel so uncomfortable there," she said. "I don't understand it. We all think up reasons to stay out all night because we don't want to come home."

As she talked, I looked clairvoyantly at the energy of her apartment. Anger! It pervaded the whole place, along with at least a dozen beings, none of whom wanted Beth and her daughters to live there. These beings had moved in with the previous tenants, out-of-control trance mediums whose idea of a pleasant evening at home had been to have screaming arguments, each competing with the other to see who could bring the worst being through his space. This couple had been evicted for excessive noise and destruction but the beings had remained and were presently working on getting Beth and her daughters evicted too.

"Would you like a house healing?" I asked Beth.

"Yes!"

So I went to work and removed no less than fifteen angry beings from her apartment, then grounded it and brought it into present time, and into affinity with her and her daughters.

A few weeks later, Beth was back at the Institute to start a class. When she saw me, she ran over and gave me a huge hug! "My apartment feels totally different!" she exclaimed. "When I got home that night, I almost turned around and left again because I thought I must be in the wrong apartment!"

I laughed. "Great! Do your daughters feel more at home too?"

"Oh, yes! When I got home, Martha, my older daughter, was watching TV. She jumped up and ran over to me and said that at 9:45 something amazing had happened to the apartment. She couldn't say exactly what—but that was the time you were doing the house healing! Anyway, she was so excited about it that she couldn't sleep, so she stayed up watching TV waiting for me to come home.

The next morning, Jan, my younger daughter, who had been asleep during the time of the healing, was very pleased because she said for the first time since we moved in there, her ears hadn't rung. I remembered you saying that ringing in your ears is often beings trying to talk to you, so now I know that all the beings are gone!"

Beth not only owned her home for the first time and felt happy in it, she invited me to come to dinner!

Rev. Sharon Wilson

DON'T PULL THE TRIGGER!

One day at work, I looked out the front window and saw several police cars careening around in a chase. As I watched, the policemen all jumped out of their cars and closed in on a man in the parking lot across the street from me.

Suddenly, my awareness changed; the world was in slow motion and my attention centered on the policeman in the lead position. He was on one knee with gun drawn and arm extended full length. Like a movie camera, my attention zoomed in on his hand holding the gun. His thumb had cocked it and his finger was poised to pull the trigger. I could clairvoyantly see the adrenalin level in his body—it was so high that he had lost control of himself. I became aware of exploring his head, locating the circuit where the message was traveling to his brain saying "There he is—shoot him!" Before the signal went to his finger telling it to pull on the trigger, I stopped it; the circuit died and his finger fell.

The man was arrested without being shot. The rest of the day, I marvelled at what I had done.

Rev. Mary Miller Fulton

I DID IT MYSELF!

I was taking quarts of cranberry juice, parsley tea and rest as a home remedy for my chronic bladder infections. I hated taking Gantricin (a sulfa drug similar to the kind that had been prescribed for me since I was eleven years old). I wanted to heal myself without drugs. I was also very tired of doctors. The last urologist at UC Medical Center told me that I probably had a structural problem and needed surgery. That statement drove me to folk medicine, and eventually to the Berkeley Psychic Institute.

In 1973 I took Rev. Ken Burke's Beginning Healing Class at BPI and was given several psychic tools to practice at home: grounding, being in the center of my head, psychic roses for protection, running life force energy and sending and receiving energy. I was also given two spiritual healing guides, one a "psychic surgeon." Rev. Ken Burke taught me how to communicate with these guides and get specific work done on my body. Using all my psychic tools I created a daily ritual of working with my healing guides. Within six weeks my urinary problem of eighteen years was gone as were any further symptoms of bladder or urinary tract infections or kidney infections. I have not even had an inflammation in more than twelve years.

No more stockpiling of cranberry juice and parsley tea! I avoided surgery and created a miracle. Nobody did it for me; instead BPI taught me how to do it myself.

Rt. Rev. Susan Hull Bostwick

HOSTAGES

"W e interrupt this program to bring you a special news bulletin." I was engrossed in buying apples from a Sebastopol fruit stand and barely heard the announcer. "Hostages . . . since 12:00 noon . . . cordoned off. . . ."

I drove back to work at the Berkeley Psychic Institute of Santa Rosa. It was 3:00 p.m. when I walked through the door, munching on my fresh Gravenstein apple.

"Anything exciting happening?" I asked the receptionist. The phone rang and I picked it up.

"Hello?" said a familiar voice. "Is this Cathy?"

"Yes, is that you, Bob?" Bob is a good friend of mine who worked at an alarm company in a building by the fairground. "Listen, I can't talk long. The police have cordoned off the office and are using all the phone lines. Some guy is holding two people hostage in the office just across from us and he has been firing shots at random. The police aren't having any luck and he's been in there since 12:00 noon. They think he's going to shoot one of the hostages. Do you think you could do something about it from there?"

Bob knew I was a healer, and in spite of his doubts about

psychics, knew that I could change situations with my psychic tools. "I'll see what I can do," I replied and hung up. My watch read 3:05 p.m.

I went into the main room of the Institute and saw one of the students there, running her energy. "Carol, how would you like to take a look at a hostage situation?"

We sat down side-by-side, went into a light trance, and soon the hostage drama was unfolding on our reading screens. I could see the gunman was drunk and had little connection as a spirit to his body. Another being was operating it, pulling the strings like a puppet. Each time a string was pulled he became angry and thought that if he hurt one of the hostages, the pain and discomfort in his body would go away.

Carol also saw the gunman's wife and child in his space, punishing him for not being a success.

We decided to go to work. "Carol, you work on the wife and child, and I'll work on the other being," I said.

Carol started making separations between the gunman's energy and that of his wife and child. She grounded them out of his space and put them back into their own bodies. While she was doing that, I grounded out the energy and control of the being that was manipulating the gunman. The police were expecting a killing and their anxiety, along with the fear of the others in the building, was in turn increasing the fear and anger of the gunman.

So I grounded the entire scene—office, hostages, gunman, police and bystanders, and started to sprinkle buckets of gold, glittering amusement over everything and everyone. At this point I saw the gunman become aware of what he was doing and start to panic. He started thinking about going to jail and fear filled his space; then he thought about ending it all right there and killing himself.

"Carol, will you put your hand on my knee and keep me grounded? I'm going to leave my body and go over there."

I felt her ground me. With my body safe, I left it, and as spirit, I placed myself in front of the gunman. "You don't have to kill yourself just because you made a mistake," I said to him, on a being level. "You can forgive yourself and end what you started." He understood me and moved in closer to his body. He started wondering what to do with his gun, but knowing that he would not now use it, I put my attention on the hostages.

As I started to tell them that it would soon be over, I realized that I knew both of them. One had been my employer for a brief period of time and the other had brought his entire family to a Psychic Fair we had sponsored. The one who had come to the Psychic Fair was a rugged, "salt of the earth" type, who wanted to own his own farm. He had been very impressed with his psychic readings that day, and before leaving had told me: "I don't know how you do it but the information I got today is going to change my life. You people keep doing what you are doing." Well, here I was, still doing what I was doing, and this time, perhaps it had saved his life!

I returned to my body, came out of trance and said: "I think it's over now." It was 3:30 p.m.

At 3:40 p.m. the phone rang. It was Bob. "Ten minutes ago the gunman threw his gun into the wastebasket and walked out!" he said. "It's over now. Thank you; I could tell you were working on it."

I later discovered that at 3:16 p.m., about the time I saw him afraid of going to jail, he had started yelling, "I'll never go back to jail!" and the hostages had thought for sure they were going to die. The newspaper also reported that the gunman had a wife and small child and had been in trouble for child abuse.

It was all pretty amazing and validating. Who says the life of a psychic is dull?

Rev. Cathy Langlois

"OH YE OF LITTLE FAITH"

Two years ago at Christmastime I helped my friend, Josie, move back to her parents' house in Oregon. My brother Mike and I filled up my car with all of her stuff and drove through sleeting rain and snow. The weather was so bad and the roads so icy that we had to spend Christmas Eve in a motel in Weed, California. The next night we arrived in Bend, Oregon and were drawing very close to her parents' home when suddenly the alternator light went on, the radio stopped playing, the heater stopped blowing, and the windshield wipers stopped wiping. The car came to a complete stop and would not start again.

Well, that didn't scare me, I knew how to fix my car, I had done it lots of times! I told Mike and Josie to hold on and I would have my healing guides heal my battery, and we would be home in no time. I grounded the car and the battery and had my healing guides change the energy of the battery to gold—and you know what? I turned the key in the ignition and NOTHING HAPPENED! Just a click—no lights, no music, no engine turning over . . . I was not having much success!

Josie said "Sue, look, we are close enough to my parents' house, Mike and I will walk there and get their car and come back with jumper cables." I was amused as they argued for braving the freezing weather, sleet and snow. I wasn't going out there because I knew I could get the car started; but they were off before I could protest.

As soon as they left I cleaned out their disbelief energy. I pointed out the electric poles of the battery to my healing guides and had them clean off the energy. In about two minutes my guides told me they were done and that I should start the car. I turned the ignition key and the motor turned over.

When I arrived at Josie's parents' house with my heater blazing, she and my brother, soaked to the skin, were just about to get into the car and come after me. The initial look on their faces was shock. Then Josie said, "What happened, did someone pass by and give you a jump already?" I just smiled and said, "I told you I could do it!"

Rev. Sue Strzelecki Gimpel

THE $30,000 MOCK-UP

T he K-M deal was a biggie. K-M was a business I had been working with for a long time, configuring a business computer system with all the whistles and bells. Things were proceeding nicely and the eleventh hour had arrived. All of a sudden, no communication. I took a clairvoyant peek at the situation. I saw that another party was being considered as the final consultant. Mr. K was being thrown a lot of invalidation because he was allowing Ms. M to make the final decisions. I also found that my female energy was rampaging through it all. Pretty amusing. I meditated and created an energy connection between Mr. K and the Supreme Being, grounded off my female energy, and sent out a neutral hello to everyone.

That cleaned off the energy and the next day I got a call that we were ready to go. Things proceeded; the system was configured, and approved.

Then another stall. No final order, no check. This was a big deal for me because Christmas was approaching and I had counted on this contract as income for the holidays. I began to wonder if you can make a good Christmas casserole out of beans and rice.

Then I remembered I was psychic and I took another look—at Ms. M this time. Well, Ms. M. was pretty sensitive, and across her shoulders she was feeling the responsibility not only for her own company, but for me, my son, and our Christmas as well. There she sat, paralyzed by energy. No wonder things were stalled. So I drained all my energy off her shoulders, separated our energies, and sent a neutral acknowledgement to her as a spirit. Two hours later the phone rang, and four hours later I had a check for $30,000. It was a Merry Christmas.

Rev. Carolyn Gregory

JUICE AND CRACKERS

1 had a mock-up to teach Sunday School. Someone had said, "If you teach Sunday School, you have a chance to get rid of the programming you received as a child when you went to Sunday School." I thought that sounded pretty terrific. So I made this mock-up and forgot about it.

In Santa Rosa, we had a new church building, with a parish house next door, and it all needed a lot of work. In the first year we had the property, we painted and improved the church itself, but did nothing on the house. When the day came for the first anniversary of the Dedication of the Grounds, we had a sunny day and a large crowd of people. There were twenty children for Sunday School and the pastor, Ross, said to me, "Marcia, could you help with the children today?"

I was delighted, but somewhat at a loss, never having taught Sunday School before, or dealt with so many children at once. It was to be in the house next door. I walked into that house and it was empty! Just bare walls. The only furniture was one end-table; there were no shelves, curtains, mats, toys, books, or any of the things you might want to have around when looking after twenty children.

Pretty soon, someone came over from the kitchen in the church and handed me a pitcher of juice and some paper cups. "You'll need these," she said, and disappeared. So we had an end-table, a pitcher of juice and some cups. Period.

I hung my coat up on a nail in the wall and looked around at the milling children. They ranged in age from about two to nine. Rosanna was there too. I knew her only slightly. She was the pre-school teacher during the week at the Yin Yang Seminary for children held at the Santa Rosa Institute. Soon she had the children sitting on the floor in a circle and she produced a children's Bible she carried in her car and read them the story of Noah and the Ark. They had lots of enthusiasm and opinions to offer and after a discussion, Danny, a plump five-year-old, said loudly, "I'm hungry!"

I looked at our pitcher of juice and thought, "Oh dear, we have no crackers!"

"I'm so hungry!" said Danny again, and I could see that his mid-morning snacks were more than a minor detail to him.

"Yes, I can see you are very hungry!" I answered. "But we haven't got any crackers today. Just juice."

"We haven't got any crackers!" some of the children repeated in dismay. "No crackers today!"

"Do you think you might have some in your car?" I asked Rosanna. She got up. "I might," she said, and went outside.

We were all in the front room of the house with the doors shut and nothing but bare walls. The children jumped around a bit and played in little groups.

This is not like Sunday School when I was a kid! I thought in amusement. Many of these children went to the Yin Yang Seminary and I knew some of them and their parents, who were students at the Berkeley Psychic Institute. They were a lively lot, with lots of confidence and also with lots of sensitivity. Psychic children. I looked around at Mandy, aged six, whom I knew a little; she was standing near my coat. Just as I looked at her, she said, "Oh, I have some crackers here!" She held out her hand. I saw a whoosh of gold energy move into her outstretched hand, and there was a packet of graham crackers. They were wrapped in paper but not in any box. She beamed and held them out to me. I was transfixed. Before I could move, the child next to her, Lisa, also aged six, said, "I have some too!" and she held out her hand. Again, a whoosh of gold energy, and she too was holding a packet of graham crackers.

Now I understood what it meant to say, "I couldn't believe my eyes!" I knew there had been no crackers in that building! The kitchen was totally empty, and anyway, we were enclosed in the front room and no one had left except Rosanna. And I knew there was nothing in or near my coat except the bare wall. I stared at these children in shock, thinking, "They've done it! They've materialized those crackers!"

"Can we be the cracker girls?" asked Mandy, smiling.

"Er . . . yes . . ." I mumbled. "I don't see why not. . . ." So they started carefully placing two crackers around for each child and pouring juice in the cups. For them it was fun, but not an extraordinary event. Soon Rosanna returned, holding a box of graham crackers.

"Look," I started to say, "You're not going to believe this, but . . ." I saw her eyes move to Mandy and Lisa passing out their crackers. I waited for her face to register surprise. She just smiled.

"Now we have lots of crackers!" cried some of the children, taking Rosanna's box and passing it to Mandy and Lisa.

"Yes, indeed we do," said Rosanna, smiling at me. She knew these children better than I did!

We all sat down for our snack and my crackers were from Mandy's packet. I tasted one carefully. It tasted real. Did I want to get rid of my Sunday School programming? I asked myself in a daze, munching on my crackers. I think I just made a good start on that!

Rev. Marcia Manix

LEWIS'S BIO

Lewis S. Bostwick was born Lewis O. Stewart May 30, 1918, in San Francisco. His astrologer father, Oliver Stewart, took off within a few years and never knew that he had a son who regularly saw rings of color and shimmerings of energy vibrations around people's bodies, predicted neighborhood events accurately and later consciously created thousands of healing miracles. He became Bostwick when his mother remarried.

As a child Lewis assumed that all people saw auras and knew that things were going to happen before they occurred. He was always getting into trouble with his precognition: he predicted the death of a neighbor to his mother's disbelief until the hearse pulled up the next day. He predicted that a fire would destroy a house because of faulty installation of a heating unit, and it burned down. Gradually, he began to realize that he was special. He has seen spontaneous combustion of a human being. He saw a black man's hair turn completely white because of having met Lewis on the astral; Lewis had teleported and sat on the edge of the man's bed in the middle of the night for ten minutes. Mysteriously, he was greeted and led away by some unknown natives to see psychic surgeons upon his arrival in the Philippines during World War II. He was to witness the first training sessions of psychic surgeons and along the way they stopped at a monastery. It was here that rose petals had fallen the night before embossed with the image of the Virgin Mary. They told him he was being taken to see the psychic surgery because he had been "called" by one of the ladies who were training the psychic surgeons.

The list of strange occurrences and miracles goes on and on. The greatest miracle of all is perhaps his creation in 1972 of his own sanctuary for other sensitive people, The Church of Divine

Man and the Berkeley Psychic Institute. Lewis had been putting together this unique church all his life. His own search took him to India and Tibet, Russia and Africa. He joined the Rosicrucians, learned from L. Ron Hubbard, joined other mystical groups and simply struck out on his own to heal, teach and study. He collated all he had learned and forged his own tools and techniques for obtaining one's spiritual freedom. Grounding, running life force energy, blowing roses, matching energy, reading from neutrality and amusement, going to the akashic records, communicating spirit to spirit are the names given to the main teachings Lewis has developed for clairvoyant training.

During the past thirteen years his teachings have touched more than 200,000 people at the nine Berkeley Psychic Institutes in California and the sister church and Washington Psychic Institutes in Washington state. More than 1,600 psychics have been graduated as ministers with 40,000 students having completed beginning meditation classes. The number of people interested in psychic development has steadily increased.

He founded the Deja Vu Publishing Company to produce all the literature of the Berkeley Psychic Institute and the Church; its monthly newspaper, The Psychic Reader, with a press run of 60,000, is the only newspaper written by psychics for psychics. It is a free general circulation paper with a pull-out BPI supplement. He is the founder and impetus behind the Aesclepion Healing Center, sponsor of the following: Trance Medium Abaton training program for trance mediums and channeling; the Nurses Healing Center, the foremost bay area training center for psychic healing for nurses; and the Marin Birth Center.

Lewis Bostwick is also a designer of fine jewelry, and formerly a watchmaker and business owner. When he isn't lecturing ("You May Be Psychic Not Crazy") throughout the San Francisco Bay Area, he conducts world-wide past life pilgrimages; Egypt, Greece, Turkey, China, and Thailand with upcoming trips to Europe and Peru. He has semi-retired to his Sonoma County home where he raises sheep, rabbits and chickens. He is the father of four daughters, two grown, Jeanne A. Jackson and Linda J. Bostwick, plus nine-year-old Dawn Rose and eleven-year-old Lili Alice by his second wife, Susan. He is an avid reader of science fiction, a stamp collector and an amateur astronomer.

Susan Hull Bostwick
Calistoga, 1987

CREED OF THE CHURCH OF DIVINE MAN

We of the Church believe in limitless space, timeless endurance, never-ending acceptance, everlasting patience and continuous comprehension. "What if a man gain the whole world and lose his own soul," asks Jesus. To a mystic, with eyes turned inward to infinity and Cosmic Consciousness, His words have great meaning. Psychic freedom creates no ideologies, no "isms," no dissenting philosophies which divide, corrupt and destroy communication between human souls. No governments are upturned, no faiths cut down by the sword, no sects or types eliminated; only a one-to-one contact between the cosmic and a living soul, which flames quietly, bringing a lifetime of contentment and a realization that nothing in this world is worth exchanging for that attainment.

CAN EVERYONE CREATE A MIRACLE?

Words & Music by
Jennifer Kimberley
Copyright ©1987

GLOSSARY

Akashic Records: *Located in the cosmos; the center for the evolutionary records of each being in the universe.*

Akashic Record Keeper: *A being whose job is to be the librarian for a person's Akashic Records.*

Astral: *The astral plane. A non-physical area where spirit exists outside of the body.*

Aura: *The energy of spirit emanating from the body; often seen in bands or layers of colors.*

Baby Beings: *Spirits who are ready to reincarnate.*

Baby-making Machinery: *The ovaries, uterus and the creative energy that powers them.*

Blowing Roses: *Psychic technique for releasing or removing energy.*

Center Chair: *The person who reads the aura and leads a clairvoyant reading.*

Center of Head: *That space in which you the spirit are most aware in the body; located behind the eyes.*

Chakra: *Sanskrit term meaning "wheel," symbolizing energy vortexes in the body, from the crown to the arches of the feet.*

Clairvoyance: *Literally, "to see clearly." The ability to see energy, auras, symbols, etc.*

Cord: *An energy connection.*

Energy Level: *Specific vibration of the aura that can be seen as color. Often described as "being in amusement," "being in survival," "being in apathy," etc.*

Female Creative Energy: *An energy that sits in front of the* abdomen in women, which can be used to create babies or other projects.

Foreign Energy: Energy that doesn't belong to you.

God of Your Heart: That part of each of us that is God, where we can find our own answers.

Grounding: An energy connection to the planet.

Growth Period: A period of change for the body that is caused by a spiritual breakthrough.

Havingness: The state in which a spirit can have.

Healing: The action of a spirit creating change in the body, either its own or someone else's.

Healing Guide: A spirit without a body who works in conjunction with a spirit with a body for the purpose of healing.

Hello: An acknowledgement of spirit.

Hooking up to the Supreme Being: Making a connection between a spirit or object and the Supreme Being.

House Control: A psychic person who makes sure that the energy within a BPI is "safe"—a comfortable place to be.

Kundalini: A healing body energy running up the spine which is very effective for moving out 'space invaders.' When out of control it is mistaken for menopause, incurable diseases, nervous disorders, etc.

Long-distance Healing: Performing a healing on someone who is not present.

Maria: A special kind of spirit, usually assigned by the Supreme Being, for protection or assistance.

Matching Energy: The ability to vibrate at the same level.

Mock-up: A creation in the formative stages.

Next Step: The next stage in growth for a spirit.

Out-of-body Healing: When a healer leaves his/her body and enters another body to perform a healing.

Past-life Aura: An aura located behind the body which contains information from past lives.

Picture: A mental image or concept.

Present Time: Now; not the past or future.

Protection Rose: A psychic tool used for safety.

Psychic Surgeon: A spirit guide that specializes in physical healing.

Reading: *Using clairvoyance to see spirit or spirit energy.*

Reading Line: *One or more people sitting in a straight line who perform a clairvoyant reading.*

Running Energy: *A technique taught at the Berkeley Psychic Institute to reclaim your life force energy.*

Seniority: *Being the most important person in your universe.*

Side Chair: *The person who sits next to the center chair in a clairvoyant reading line and who performs part of the reading.*

Space: *A term defining the aura and the body; personal territory.*

Supreme Being: *God. Creator.*

.

LOCATIONS OF THE BERKELEY PSYCHIC INSTITUTES

Of Berkeley
2436 Haste Street
Berkeley, Ca. 94704
(415) 548-8020

Of Marin
1752 Lincoln Avenue
San Rafael, Ca. 94901
(415) 459-8830

Of Palo Alto
235 Alma Street
Palo Alto, Ca. 95407
(415) 325-4124

Of Pleasanton
328 St. Mary's Street
Pleasanton, Ca.
94566
(415) 462-3040

Of Sacramento
1614 27th Street
Sacramento, Ca. 95816
(916) 452-4081

Of San Diego
3137 Nimitz Boulevard
San Diego, Ca. 92106
(619) 224-1797

Of San Jose
180 E. Younger Avenue
San Jose, Ca. 95113
(408) 298-6443

Of Santa Rosa
520 Sonoma Avenue
Santa Rosa, Ca. 95401
(707) 545-8891

Santa Cruz Mission
1320 Mission Street
Santa Cruz, Ca. 95060
(408) 429-6166